SHAKESPEARE AND THE TEMPEST

SHAKESPEARE AND THE TEMPEST

By

FRANCIS NEILSON

RICHARD R. SMITH PUBLISHER, INC.

Rindge, New Hampshire

1956

Published by Richard R. Smith Publisher, Inc.
Topside, West Rindge, New Hampshire

Library of Congress Catalog Card Number: 56-9168

Set up, printed and bound in
the United States of America by
The Colonial Press Inc.

To the memory of
Edward Dowden and George Brandes,
my earliest mentors,
and to my dear friends,
Sir Johnston Forbes-Robertson
and Walter Hampden

CONTENTS

SHAKESPEARE AND THE TEMPEST

THE REASON
FOR THIS STUDY

THERE ARE MANY biographical and critical works about our poet and his plays. They have come from authors of nearly every country in Europe as well as America, and each year a new one is added to the long list. For over fifty years I have read many of their volumes. One of the first to fascinate me was *William Shakespeare, A Critical Study*, by George Brandes. The translation was first published in 1898, but my copy bore the date of 1901. It was left behind in England when I departed for America in 1915. The loss was incalculable to me, for upon nearly every page I had set down marginal notes.

My present copy bears the date of 1914. It was the eighth edition of the work. To say that it took the English scholars by storm is putting it mildly. The *Athenaeum* said: "No other single work on Shakespeare includes so much, and so much that is valuable." The *Spectator* called it "a great book."

It is all that, even though we know much more about Shakespeare now than scholars did two generations ago. Brandes startled many of our sleepy critics of dramatic literature when he said:

> Shakespeare stands co-equal with Michael Angelo
> in pathos and with Cervantes in humour. This of itself

gives us a certain standard for measuring the height and range of his powers.[1]

Since the publication of Brandes' famous study, brilliant schools of Elizabethan scholars have contributed invaluable treatises upon the plays as they are read; the sources from which Shakespeare took his plots, and, also, the hundred and one problems concerned with authorship, style, versification and characterization. But not one of any consequence treats the plays from the standpoint of the man who has to produce them. The commentaries I have read make their appeal directly to a reader. Hence, the many errors that arise, such as those that I have pointed out in my humble contributions: *Hamlet and Shakespeare* and *A Study of Macbeth for the Stage.*[2]

In dealing with *The Tempest*, I intend to consider it as a piece to be performed in a theater, where the educated congregate together with Tom, Dick and Harry. It is there the folk of the pit and the gallery (groundlings, if you prefer the term) see the piece with those who can afford to pay for a stall or a box.

If the play under consideration is to be understood by the scholar in the library and the stage director in the theater, it is necessary to go very deeply into the life of the author, the creator of Prospero. The reason for this is that critics have decided it is the only piece by Shakespeare which gives an insight into the mind of the poet. Some see in it an autobiographical trend, which, of course, would never be noticed by one witnessing its production on the stage.

But this idea is important also because it leads us to wonder why, after the amazing achievement of writing the last tragedies, he turned his mind to a play of redemption. We might

[1] *Op. cit.* (London: William Heinemann), p. 1.
[2] These books were privately printed and distributed in 1950 and 1952 respectively. Many copies were given to public and university libraries throughout the United States.

ask ourselves how much of Shakespeare is in Prospero, and in what way do their ideas resemble each other? We cannot possibly fathom this surprising change in thought unless we know more of the history of the author than our Shakespearian scholars have presented to us. To my mind, there is a world of observation and experience that lies behind the writing of this strange, eventful story, and which cannot be dissociated from the period in which he and his parents lived. The events—economic, political and religious—that took place in England from the time of the coming of the Tudors until the advent of the Stuarts, were so calamitous that no thoughtful person, whether or not he was able to read or write, could be impervious to it; for it affected every class in the kingdom and brought about horrors worse than war.

It is my purpose in this study to show the spiritual effect upon Shakespeare of the great changes in the law and custom of the land, which had taken place in the lives of his grandfather, his father and himself. I hope to illustrate how these were indelibly imprinted upon his mind when he was a pupil at the grammar school in Stratford.

The plan of this study has intentionally been a fluid one, in which the reader may find some repetitions and digressions. However, I feel I have something to say that may be of interest, and I shall present facts about the Tudor period that have been overlooked by many of the critics.

The Arden edition of *The Tempest*, with an introduction by Frank Kermode,[3] is one of the most elaborate studies of the play I have read. The ground he covers is so extensive, and the abundance of detail so vast, that it is not easy to absorb it all in one reading. Yet, the thought crosses one's mind, if Shakespeare were with us today, would he not be mightily puzzled to know what to make of it all? For there were no library critics in his day. He wrote the plays to be

[3] Fifth edition; London: Methuen & Co., 1954.

acted before an audience, either at court or on the boards of the Globe or some other theater. They were presented with costume and properties, but with little attempt at scenery, such as that provided by modern productions.

It should be remembered that the audience saw the actors in action and heard them speak. Ninety-five per cent of them would not know anything about the technical construction of the lines, whether they were poetry or prose; for the spoken line is something quite different from that which is read in the study. The reader with the book in his hand sees at once the form, because his eye is cast over the page; but there is no page for a man sitting in the theater.

I have known actors who have so transmogrified Shakespeare's verse that it has lost all poetic rhythm. Henry Irving, in *The Merchant of Venice* and in *Macbeth*, would break a sentence with a pause to cast a look or to make a gesture. Sometimes he would throw in a "Bah!" At other times, to add touches to the character, he would cough slightly or twist his head or limbs, to emphasize the peculiar nature of the part. Indeed, it may be said that all these acting tricks, not set down in the stage directions of the plays, were hallmarks of the actor's technique of presenting his own version of the character.

What did he think or care about sources or about the different forms of verse, as the expert in poetry understands them? What did he know of iambic pentameter or even a verse of only five measures? I have met and worked with many of the leading actors of the past sixty years, but I do not recollect discussing with one the forms of verse used by Shakespeare in his plays. Forbes-Robertson and Walter Hampden were probably the only men who were inclined to go more deeply into a play as a whole than those who studied only a part to be performed.

It is a pity we know so little about the methods of rehearsal of these plays when they were first presented. A prompt book made by Shakespeare has not yet been discovered, and this fact makes us wonder from what script the actors studied their parts. Was the play as a whole read to the company by the author, and afterwards, did each actor write out his own part, with cues, from the manuscript? That would be an arduous business and take a lot of time. It certainly could not have been done in the cast of *Twelfth Night*, if Dr. Leslie Hotson's story[4] of its production is to be accepted, for it was written and produced in great haste. Therefore, we can imagine what a busy time the prompter must have had at the first performance. We find it difficult to visualize what took place, then, during the rehearsals of a new play.

In Heminge and Condell's First Folio, the meager stage directions do not answer the purpose of a prompt book. Such instructions as we find in the plays—entrances and exits, music cues, thunder and lightning—are only what a stage novice would mark. In the prompt book of a skilled producer the positions of the actors in the scene would call for precise instructions, and add perhaps ten or a dozen pages to the script.

When I began as an actor, stage managers were rough-and-ready gentlemen, and I never remember one reading a play to the company. Parts were distributed to each actor and actress, and sometimes they did not know the plot of the play, or the denouement, until they had rehearsed the whole of it once. Even then, they were by no means letter perfect, and weeks of repetition were necessary before some of them grasped the nature of the roles they had to play. Indeed, in many plays that I produced, actors learned the dialogue at rehearsal while acting the intricate business of the scene.

Only once have I attended a rehearsal at which each actor held the complete play in his hand. That was at the Schaus-

[4] *The First Night of Twelfth Night* (N.Y.: Macmillan Co., 1954).

pielhaus in Munich, when I was invited to see the first performance of Maeterlinck's *Monna Vanna.* It was a novel experience for me, for I had never produced a play that had
been published.

Nowadays any company desiring to perform a play of
Shakespeare has no difficulty in providing each actor with
a copy. In some cases it is possible, through French's editions of the plays, to use prompt copies that have done service for the productions given by famous actors.

To think back to the days when Shakespeare introduced
a new play to his company calls for the imagination of a
highly qualified stage director. He stands in a different
sphere of art from that of the literary expert, who gives us
erudite essays on the source, the construction, and the literary technique of his plays.

The reader must not think for a moment that I do not
value highly most of the critical analyses that have enriched
the literature on Shakespeare. My wish is only to mark
definitely the difference—the wide one—that lies between
the work of the Shakespearian expert and that of the stage
director. The one belongs to the library and the study; the
other to the theater, for he is to rehearse the actors. The
first appeals to a reader; the other is conscious, first and last,
that the appeal is to be made to an auditor. Therefore, when
I question the benefit of all this excellent work of the essay-
ists to the producer and the actor, I am merely trying to
differentiate clearly between the functions of the literary
expert and the man who has to produce the play.

I am prepared to admit that my intrusion into the realm
of Shakespearian scholarship may be regarded by the critics,
who are purists, as arrogance on the part of a critic who has
no academic footing. It is a bold adventure for one who, in
this study, will clash with the opinion of some of the writers
who have given us invaluable information on sources, literary technique, and biographical information about the poet.

But whether or not a stage director, a man of the theater, is highly esteemed by the academicians, he may make an appeal to all those students who are interested in the plays from the standpoint of the theatergoer. After all, they are the judges of the worth of a production.

This study, then, falls into two parts: (1) a review of the social and constitutional changes that were taking place under the Tudors and how they molded the mind of the man who wrote *The Tempest;* and (2) an analysis of the play itself, considering the technical problems of staging it in the theater.

Two

THE HOUSE OF TUDOR

THE DEFEAT AT Bosworth and death of the last king of
the line of York, in 1485, hastened the end of a period that
had been in decline for nearly a century. It was the final
battle of the Wars of the Roses, the struggle between the
Houses of Lancaster and of York, and brought to the throne
of England a man of Welsh descent, who was dubbed a bastard, for no record has been found of a marriage between
his father and the widow of Henry V.

Already many changes had been wrought in the law and
custom of the land; there were more yet to come, which
would be deeply and sorely felt by the people. Much of this
aspect has been neglected by the recorders, but since the
middle of the last century records have been unearthed
which were unknown to the historians of earlier periods, and
from them we gather facts that are new.

To what extent the knowledge of these changes affected
the literary and spiritual mind of Shakespeare has not been
weighed as seriously as the subject deserves. In many respects, this matter touches the question of his education.
Concerning it we are now in a position to maintain that, in
Stratford, there was no reason why he should have been a
dull pupil. There was an excellent free grammar school open
to boys, and the available literature, pagan and Christian—
catalogued by some of the experts—would compare favor-
ably with what can now be found in a small-town library.

One fact that has been overlooked by some recorders is

that a Reformation was taking place in England when Martin Luther was a young boy. The revolt began within and without the Church, and it was fostered in the universities. The men who were responsible for starting this reform were the giants of learning of that day. Linacre was born some twenty years before Luther; Colet some sixteen years before; Thomas More was of the same period; and Grocyn was about thirty-seven years older than Luther. These were some of the men—all Englishmen—who were concerned in reforms within the Church, and who broke the almost sterile discipline of the schoolmen of a dying age. The reformers of the early years of Henry VII were responsible for the revival of learning, and threw the doors of knowledge open to the people themselves.

It is amazing to go through the list of works which these men brought to the notice of the English. The printing presses were busy in the principal countries of Europe. It is estimated that ten thousand editions of books and pamphlets were published in the last thirty years of the fifteenth century. This astonishing change rang the curtain down upon the last dark days of medieval restriction. Suddenly much of the literature of the past was available for any grammar school boy to study. All this was taking place about a century before William Shakespeare was born.

It is well for us to look into the history of England during the Tudor period, for in the plays there is much evidence that Shakespeare was aware of certain grave changes that have been touched upon only lightly by the historians of our time. He must have had the investigator's eye for, as we shall see, there was little of moment that took place in the towns or along the country roads that escaped his notice. His apprenticeship, during what have been called the "lost years," indicates clearly that he was born to be a historian of singular genius. One has only to read carefully *Henry VI, Part I*, to be convinced of this. How long he worked upon this play no one knows, but it bears the imprint of careful study. It is generally accepted by the scholars that the material was found in the *Chronicles* of Halle and Holinshed. And some are under the impression that he studied these sources long before he went to London, to become known as an actor of importance.

The story told by Alan Keen and Roger Lubbock, in *The Annotator*,[1] has yet to be given deep consideration by the Shakespearian experts. It tells of the discovery of a copy of Halle's *Chronicle*, thickly annotated in the margin by a hand of Shakespeare's time. I have spent much thought on the problem arising from this discovery, for I have long held the notion that Shakespeare was at heart a radical constitutionalist, and implicitly believed in all that is implied in the phrase "the law and custom of the land."

There are many passages in the plays that substantiate this idea. To him the coming of the Tudors meant much more than a mere change of reigning houses:

Hung be the heavens with black, yield day to night!
Comets, importing change of times and states,
Brandish your crystal tresses in the sky,
And with them scourge the bad revolting stars. . . . .[2]

Another prophecy is:

Posterity, await for wretched years,
When at their mothers' moist eyes babes shall suck. . . . .[3]

These lines are in the earliest scenes he wrote, and there is, too, the first evidence of a theme that runs through several of his other plays:

[1] London: Putnam, 1954.
[2] *1 Henry VI*, Act I, scene 3. (The quotations from all plays except *The Tempest* are taken from *The Oxford Shakespeare*, ed. by W. J. Craig [Oxford University Press, 1925].)
[3] *Ibid.*

> . . . . Thou most usurping proditor,
> And not protector, of the king or realm.[4]

"Usurper!" To him usurpers were all bad men, no matter how great they were or how royal their blood. In another history, an early one, *King John* (1594),[5] we find Constance, the mother of Arthur, denouncing the King:

> . . . . But Fortune, O!
> She is corrupted, chang'd, and won from thee:
> She adulterates hourly with thine uncle John,
> And with her golden hand hath pluck'd on France
> To tread down fair respect of sovereignty,
> And made his majesty the bawd to theirs.
> France is a bawd to Fortune and King John,
> That strumpet Fortune, that usurping John![6]

Who can doubt the close study Shakespeare must have given to the history of his land, when we have in mind the dramas of her kings he based upon the knowledge then extant? To bring convincing evidence of this fact, I shall have to resort later to other plays which mark dynastic changes, but the trilogy of the Plantagenets suffices for the purpose of establishing this fact.

Can we assume, then, that Shakespeare, having read so deeply in the chronicles of the period, was a student Prospero, searching for an Ariel who would help him in some supernatural way to right the wrongs of the time? Supernatural it would have to be, for he had learned early the impotence of the human being to restore order in the realm, and bring back the days of abundant harvests for a happy people.

The memory of a period when there was peace in the land is shown clearly in all the plays, and yet there is often

[4] *Ibid.*
[5] Because of the wide difference of opinion regarding the chronology of the plays, I have used the dates compiled by F. Madan for *The Oxford Shakespeare*, p. 1351.
[6] *King John*, Act III, scene 1.

a profound melancholy that underlies the thought of what had been and the conditions of life of his day. It is the same strain of melancholy that we find running through the sonnets of Michelangelo, who died just about the time Shakespeare was born. For both of them the spiritual and cultural period had passed and could never be restored through human agency.

To my mind, *Henry VI, Part I* was a kind of manual, a primer-lexicon, out of which he developed not only the history of the English dynasties, as it was then known, but the ideas he wove into themes in many of his plays.

Foul play, in all its detestable methods—bastardy, usurpation, sedition, perjury and treachery—rings the changes in the scenes of these dramas of royal dissension. The King cries out after one of the quarrels of Gloucester and Winchester:

> Believe me, Lords, my tender years can tell
> Civil dissension is a viperous worm.[7]

And Mortimer tells Richard Plantagenet:

> The first-begotten, and the lawful heir
> Of Edward king, the third of that descent:
> During whose reign the Percies of the North,
> Finding his usurpation most unjust,
> Endeavour'd my advancement to the throne.[8]

Then after the patched-up quarrel which has raged between the Bishop of Winchester and the Duke of Gloucester, uncles of the King, Exeter fears the future. He knows it is only a feigned compact that has been made between them, which "will at last break out into a flame." And then he says:

> And now I fear that fatal prophecy
> Which in the time of Henry, nam'd the Fifth,

[7] *I Henry VI*, Act III, scene 1.
[8] *Ibid.*, Act II, scene 5.

Was in the mouth of every sucking babe;
That Henry born at Monmouth should win all;
And Henry born at Windsor should lose all:
Which is so plain that Exeter doth wish
His days may finish ere that hapless time.[9]

We must remember that line: "Was in the mouth of every sucking babe." This is of vast importance, for it refers to the hearsay and legends that were passed from one hearth to another, generation after generation, by unschooled historians. These were the tales that lived in the minds of the folk. There are many examples of this in the plays, and later I shall give three or four instances of how Shakespeare used them to advantage.

The poet must have been at work upon *Henry VI* a few years before he wrote *Love's Labour's Lost* (1590), which might have been regarded at the time as a pot-boiler. Yet, what a contrast in theme and workmanship. The one, melodrama of the highest order; the other, high comedy of a quality seldom surpassed. (I use the term "melodrama" to express a type of play which was so popular in the old days of Drury Lane and the Adelphi, in which there were no songs but always incidental music.)

The division of the acts of *Henry VI* into many scenes has been one reason why it is seldom given. It is one of the most difficult for the producer to mount. Beerbohm Tree told me that he would have liked to make two separate plays of the first part of it.

Before we leave this play and pass on to the next stage of our thesis, I must quote one or two more passages that will help us to understand the attitude of Shakespeare's mind at that time. The King tells his uncle he always thought

It was both impious and unnatural
That such immanity and bloody strife
Should reign among professors of one faith.[10]

[9] *Ibid.*, Act III, scene 1.
[10] *Ibid.*, Act V, scene 1.

Then there is the prophecy of Henry V regarding Winchester:

> If once he come to be a Cardinal,
> He'll make his cap co-equal with the crown.[11]

The aside of Winchester indicates his relations with Gloucester:

> I'll either make thee stoop and bend thy knee,
> Or sack this country with a mutiny.[12]

The plays bring to us in many scenes ghosts, spirits and witches. The first intimation we have of the use of evil spirits—fiends, as they are called in this play—occurs when Joan calls on her helpers:

> Now, ye familiar spirits, that are cull'd
> Out of the powerful regions under earth
> Help me this once, that France may get the field.[13]

This play is more than an introduction to the sort of knowledge gathered by Shakespeare in his apprenticeship days; it is a kind of handbook, which gives us an understanding of how his mind was shaped by the dynastic changes of the realm.

The difference between history and legend was not so precisely drawn then as it is today. And Shakespeare undoubtedly was familiar with the stories of the long ago as they were passed down from family to family. We are far too sophisticated now to appreciate the value of the verbal recordings of the folk. Still, myth and legend cling to superstitious minds as mussels to a rock. The people of Shakespeare's day practiced pagan rites and celebrated festivals that were as old as those of Cybele. The memories were in their blood. Dr. Margaret Murray, in her amazing chronicle

[11] *Ibid.*
[12] *Ibid.*
[13] *Ibid.*, scene 3.

of *The Divine King in England*,[14] informs us that the Dianic cult was practiced in England down to the reign of the Stuarts.

But who knows now the stories of early days, which were recounted at the hearthside—stories of times when "a woman and her babe could walk scatheless from sea to sea"; when England was under the rule of Eadwine? In many scenes of the plays Shakespeare makes us aware of what the common folk gathered concerning the doings of royalty and rebels.

Examples of how quickly the news of calamity filters down to the folk is found in several of the plays. There were no newspapers or broadcasters in the day of King John, but the rumors of the death of Arthur spread rapidly among the people at Pomfret:

> Young Arthur's death is common in their mouths;
> And when they talk of him, they shake their heads
> And whisper one another in the ear;
> And he that speaks, doth gripe the hearer's wrist
> Whilst he that hears makes fearful action,
> With wrinkled brows, with nods, with rolling eyes.
> I saw a smith stand with his hammer, thus,
> The whilst his iron did on the anvil cool,
> With open mouth swallowing a tailor's news;
> Who, with his shears and measure in his hand,
> Standing on slippers, which his nimble haste
> Had falsely thrust upon contrary feet,—
> Told of a many thousand warlike French,
> That were embattailed and rank'd in Kent.
> Another lean unwash'd artificer
> Cuts off his tale and talks of Arthur's death.[15]

Earlier in the same scene the Bastard tells the King:

> But as I travell'd hither through the land,
> I find the people strangely fantasied,

[14] London: Faber and Faber, 1954.
[15] *King John*, Act IV, scene 2.

Possess'd with rumours, full of idle dreams,
Not knowing what they fear, but full of fear.[16]

One has only to read the garden scene in *Richard II* to be convinced that the common people were their own recorders. Consider this speech:

Go, bind thou up yon dangling apricocks,
Which, like unruly children, make their sire
Stoop with oppression of their prodigal weight:
Give some supportance to the bending twigs.
Go thou, and like an executioner,
Cut off the heads of too fast growing sprays,
That look too lofty in our commonwealth:
All must be even in our government.
You thus employ'd, I will go root away
The noisome weeds, that without profit suck
The soil's fertility from wholesome flowers.[17]

Could a more vivid description of the turmoil of the court be given by a historian? So often it happens in the plays that the man of the workaday world gathers information of moment, not known to his employers. Later, in the same piece, Richard's Queen learns about the conspiracy of Bolingbroke from the gardener, who advises her:

Post you to London and you'll find it so;
I speak no more than every one doth know.[18]

At this, the Queen cries out: "And am I last that knows it?"

I could quote similar instances from other scenes, but this one indicates clearly the avid mind of a gleaner who despised no source that could satisfy his hunger for what he considered to be facts.

Professor Kitson Clark, a Fellow of Trinity College, Cambridge, in his essay, *The English Inheritance*,[19] has given us

[16] *Ibid.*
[17] Act III, scene 4.
[18] *Ibid.*
[19] London: S C M Press, 1950.

examples of the persistence with which the sense of right endured in the public mind for generations. Law, in the sense of what was respected by their forefathers, was, to them, a sacred possession. Professor Clark's work is invaluable for one who is interested in studying closely the dramas I am dealing with here. He states:

> Law penetrated all things, it entered into language, into thought, into Shakespeare's plays to such an extent that that has been part of the case that they were actually written by a great lawyer, and always into politics. Lawyers penetrated everywhere. They filled the government service, they advised the opponents of government, where such were bold enough to exist, they filled the House of Commons. . . . . Small wonder that the Tudors were to accept the ancient law of England as a sturdy if barbarous ally. Small wonder that when the Stuarts stumbled against what most contemporary Englishmen imagined the law to be they were brought down into the dust.[20]

Clark recognizes, moreover, that the laws of King Edward the Confessor, in all probability, went "right back to a pre-Christian world in which for the free man there was an elaborate code of personal rights and personal obligations and a strong sense of justice."

The idea of the freedom of the individual being derived from a law of nature was the common heritage of the people in early medieval times, and our history is full of instances when the people rose in revolt against monarchs who violated their sense of what was right.

There need be no question raised about Shakespeare's knowledge of the law, even in such prosaic matters as contracts, violations of municipal ordinances, or other legal business. We shall see that William, as a quick-witted boy, had many occasions to learn from his father's predicaments the jargon of lawyers and the methods of their practice.

[20] Pp. 26-7.

Three

THE MOLDING OF
SHAKESPEARE'S MIND

IT IS NOW fairly well established by the investigators that good yeoman blood coursed in the veins of our poet. His grandfather was a farmer, but it is not known whether he was a freeholder or a tenant. At any rate, many tenants in the shires of that time were of the yeoman class.

Shakespeare's father was born at Snitterfield, and moved early in life to Stratford, four miles away. There are records of his breaking certain ordinances, and of his being fined for making a "muckhill at chamber's door." But it is not necessary here to go over the ground examined so carefully by recent scholars concerning the business and municipal troubles of John Shakespeare. In the past twenty years we have had tome after tome dealing with the new finds of the experts, and for any reader who still harbors the superficial notions held a generation ago about the poet's early life, I would recommend the volume by M. M. Reese, *Shakespeare, His World and His Work*.[1] It is one of the best biographies that has been produced in this generation.

However, there is something of importance to be considered, which has only been touched upon lightly by the recorders. It has to do with the grave economic and political happenings that were taking place in England for many years before Shakespeare was born. These are marked in the

[1] London: Edward Arnold & Co., 1953.

histories, and can easily be traced back to the days of Richard II and John of Gaunt. George Trevelyan, in *English Social History*, and Sir John Clapham, in *A Concise Economic History of England*, mention some of the events that were manifestations of the discontent of the people. But these historians treat them with a reserve—I might say a conservative appraisal—that skims over the disastrous changes suffered by the poor.

Perhaps the most reliable description we can have of the dire effect of these events is to be found in More's *Utopia*. It was written in 1516, seven years after Henry VIII came to the throne, which was about the time when Richard Shakespeare was born. In this amazing story of the work of the Kingdom of Nowhere, More declares that he considers life is nothing but "a conspiracy of the rich against the poor." It is hard to reconcile this statement with the contrast of a thriving yeomanry, prosperous towns, and a happy people, as some of our historians describe the conditions of that period. It is true there was another side to this picture; it was not all black. But More hits the nail right on the head when he says:

> . . . . And yet besides this the riche men not only by private fraud but also by commen lawes do every day pluck and snatche awaye from the poore some parte of their daily living. So whereas it seemed before unjuste to recompense with unkindnes their paynes that have bene beneficiall to the publique weale, nowe they have to this their wrong and unjuste dealinge (which is yet a muche worse pointe) geven the name of justice, yea and that by force of a lawe. Therefore when I consider and way in my mind all these commen wealthes, which now a dayes any where do florish, so god helpe me, I can perceave nothing but a certain conspiracy of riche men procuringe theire owne commodities under the name and title of the commen wealth. They invent and devise all meanes and craftes, first how to kepe safely, without feare of lesing, that

they have unjustly gathered together, and next how to hire and abuse the worke and laboure of the poore for as litle money as may be. These devises, when the riche men have decreed to be kept and observed under coloure of the comminaltie, that is to saye, also of the pore people, then they be made lawes. But these most wicked and vicious men, when they have by their unsatiable covetousnes devided among them selves al those thinges, whiche woulde have sufficed all men, yet how farre be they from the welth and felicitie of the Utopian commen wealth? . . . .[2]

More did not write without his file of facts. He was the most brilliant lawyer of his day, and the statutes enacted by the Crown and Parliament were familiar to him. In *Utopia* he reveals clearly that he could trace the undoing of the English peasantry from the time when wide areas of the land were enclosed for pasture and given over to grazing sheep. It is only necessary to read the story of the insurrections that brought about the Statute of Laborers to be convinced that More's knowledge of the drastic changes in the law and custom of the land could not be questioned.

Two years after *Utopia* was published, a commission reported wholesale depopulation, houses lying waste, inhabitants departed, churches falling into ruins, and the breakup of villages. The cause of these evil conditions was the spread of sheep farming. Acts of Parliament during Henry VIII's reign confirmed this state of affairs. Hugh Latimer has given a picture of the conditions under which his father "had a farm of £3 or £4 a year" (that is, according to the rent of the land at the time, from 120 to 160 acres arable):

> On this he employed six labourers. He had walk for a hundred sheep, and his wife milked thirty cows, which also, of course, must have mainly subsisted in

[2] *Utopia*, The Temple Classics (4th ed.; London: J. M. Dent and Co., 1904), trans. by Raphe Robynson, second book, p. 158.

summer on the common pasture. . . . . He gave his daughters portions, £5 or 10 marks a piece, kept hospitality, and gave alms to the poor, from the profits of his tenance. The present farmer gives £16 a year for the same holding, and has no surplus for the king's taxes, for his own savings, for his children's advancement, or for the poor.[3]

In another of his Sermons Latimer said, "Where there was a great many of householders there is now but a shepherd and his dog."

It does not seem at all likely that Richard Shakespeare, in the remote village of Snitterfield, or thereabouts, would purchase a copy of *Utopia*. It is doubtful whether he could read, much less write. But there was a way, practiced as late as the 1870's in English villages, of learning what was said and written in the great world of educated people. It is no mystery to me how the common folk—the illiterate even—of the days of the Tudors, gathered information about royal procedures in and out of Parliament. It may be merely a story, attributed to Horace Walpole, that the revolution which brought about the Reform Act of 1832 was shaped in the cellars of the taverns of London, where men gathered to hear someone read John Wilkes' paper, the *North Briton*.

Dr. Margaret Murray gives a startling instance of the rapidity with which news circulated as early as the eleventh century. It concerns the death of William Rufus, the King:

. . . . It seems certain that the death was expected, for the news was known not only in Devonshire but in Normandy within twenty-four hours. Anselm and the abbot of Cluny claimed that the news was brought

[3] Thirty-first Sermon, in the complete edition of his works ed. by G. E. Corrie for the Parker Society, 2 vols. (London, 1844-5). Also E. Arber's ed. of Latimer's *Seven Sermons Preached Before Edward VI* (London, 1869). This quotation may be found in James E. Thorold Rogers, *Six Centuries of Work and Wages* (N.Y.: G. P. Putnam's Sons, n.d.), pp. 445-6.

by angelic messengers, whereas in England it was the Devil who was the news bringer. But it must have been by some system of preconcerted signals, such as is common among primitive peoples.[4]

A place even so remote as Snitterfield, lying at the heart of England, was not proof against rumors of the wicked events taking place in London, nor could it be left in ignorance of the risings of discontented people in many of the other shires. It is not likely that Warwickshire was exempt from the exactions of arbitrary rule, arbitrary taxation, and other impositions which not only violated the conscience of the folk, but laid upon their backs burdens hard to be borne.

Richard Shakespeare would hear in Stratford on market days the rumors that passed from town to town. The bands of strolling players who came to the inns for lodgment were purveyors of news greedily taken in by the townsfolk. We know that William Shakespeare regarded them as recorders, for in *Hamlet* he warns Polonius to see them "well bestowed," and orders him to "let them be well used; for they are the abstracts and brief chronicles of the time." [5]

And what would be the stories of their ready tongues? The King's war with France, the divorce of Queen Katharine, the trumped-up charges against Anne Boleyn, the impositions laid by Wolsey, the protestations against the levies imposed for devious purposes, such as supplies for the war, which they considered merely an excuse of the Cardinal to gather more of their wealth to add to his ill-gotten gains. Much of this is revealed in *Henry VIII*, one of the last works to which our poet's name is appended.

Whether or not Richard Shakespeare could read or write, we may be sure he missed little of the information that filtered down to the people and alarmed their souls. After

[4] *The Divine King. . . . ,* p. 59.
[5] Act II, scene 2.

the fall of Wolsey, the crimes of the Crown threatened "to o'ertop old Pelion or the skyish head of blue Olympus." John Richard Green in *A Short History of the English People* tells us:

> The ten years which follow the fall of Wolsey are among the most momentous in our history. The New Monarchy at last realized its power, and the work for which Wolsey had paved the way was carried out with a terrible thoroughness. The one great institution which could still offer resistance to the royal will was struck down. The Church became a mere instrument of the central despotism. The people learned their helplessness in rebellions easily suppressed and avenged with ruthless severity. A reign of terror, organized with consummate and merciless skill, held England panic-stricken at Henry's feet. The noblest heads rolled on the block. Virtue and learning could not save Thomas More: royal descent could not save Lady Salisbury. The putting away of one queen, the execution of another, taught England that nothing was too high for Henry's "courage" or too sacred for his "appetite." Parliament assembled only to sanction acts of unscrupulous tyranny, or to build up by its own statutes the great fabric of absolute rule. All the constitutional safeguards of English freedom were swept away. Arbitrary taxation, arbitrary legislation, arbitrary imprisonment were powers claimed without dispute and unsparingly exercized by the Crown.[6]

This is touched upon far too lightly by some of the chief historians of our day. They seem to ignore the evidence of the iniquities of the time, which is abundant in the plays.

Further historical support of this verdict is given by James E. Thorold Rogers, the historian and Member of Parliament, who published his great work, *Six Centuries of Work and Wages*, seventy years ago. In it I find this extraordinary passage:

[6] Pp. 331-2.

. . . . I contend that from 1563 to 1824, a conspiracy, concocted by the law and carried out by parties interested in its success, was entered into, to cheat the English workman of his wages, to tie him to the soil, to deprive him of hope, and to degrade him into irremediable poverty. In a subsequent chapter I shall dwell on the palliatives which were adopted in order to mitigate the worst and most intolerable burdens of his life—palliatives which were rendered necessary by no fault of his, but by the deliberate malignity of Governments and Parliaments. For more than two centuries and a half the English law, and those who administered the law, were engaged in grinding the English workman down to the lowest pittance, in stamping out every expression or act which indicated any organized discontent, and in multiplying penalties upon him when he thought of his natural rights. . . . .[7]

Mark the date, 1563—the year before Shakespeare was born!

John Shakespeare, no doubt, learned from his father about the debasement of the currency. To raise revenue for his extravagances, King Henry VIII reduced the amount of silver in the shilling. Originally it cost over elevenpence in silver, but so much alloy was introduced into it that at last it only contained three pennyworth of silver. The people refused to accept the new coinage at its face value, and no wonder, for they discovered that it cost thirty pence to buy what they formerly could purchase for tenpence. This, of course, affected wages, and the discontent deepened. A period of inflation set in and, as it increased, the purchasing power of the shilling dwindled.

In *Henry IV, Part I*, a Carrier says of Robin Ostler, "Poor fellow! never joyed since the price of oats rose; it was the death of him."[8] Yet, the experts scarcely refer to these

[7] P. 398.
[8] Act II, scene 1.

matters. From some of the scholarly works the student might gather the impression that Stratford tradesmen and laborers were enjoying fairly prosperous times when John Shakespeare left Snitterfield and settled down as a glover. That he became a man of wealth in a town of two thousand inhabitants cannot be gainsaid, for as Reese shows in his work, he was no bankrupt, although there are instances of his failing to pay his debts, and even the town dues. Strange, that such a person should remain a functionary of importance until nearly the end of his life.

If we would divine the mind of Shakespeare when he wrote *The Tempest*, it is surely necessary to inquire into that part of his education received at the hearthside. We may be sure of this: even at such a grammar school as the one at Stratford, he would not learn from the teacher much about the causes of the changes that were taking place in the law of the land. It was just as hard then as it is now, to learn in school what tricks are played by politicians before high heaven.

When, then, did the themes embodied in so many of the plays take root in his mind? Is it too much to say that Shakespeare never departed from the opinions which must have been formed when he was a boy? Of course, we can only guess at what he learned about the state of the realm. But when we turn to his earliest work, we find the zest and application of a young historian engrossed with the reign of Henry VI, and filled with forebodings of what the strife of the houses of York and Lancaster meant for England.

He was born in 1564. Malone's historical order of the plays places *Henry VI, Part I* in 1589. He was then twenty-five years old. Furnivall, however, fixes the date of this drama at 1592; so do the modern critics, who place *Love's Labour's Lost* as the first work, in 1590; the *Comedy of*

Errors in 1591; and *Henry VI, Part I* in 1592. But today we know far more about the chronology than Malone and Furnivall did.[9]

However, it is abundantly clear, from the order now accepted, that the histories dealing with the English kings were written in the period from 1592 to 1599. This, of course, does not include *Henry VIII*, which bears the date of 1611. To write nine long historical dramas on English kings within seven years surely indicates a desire on the part of the poet to go deeply into the history of his time. It so far exceeds the record we have of the output of any other poet that we are amazed at his industry.

What is the basic theme running through all the histories? Foul play! What is the theme of *The Tempest?* Foul play! Prospero tells Miranda: "By foul play, as thou sayest, were we heaved thence." In all the histories it is foul play upon which Shakespeare bases his work as a dramatist. The foul play of usurpation, of regicide, of sedition.

How is it possible to read the three parts of *Henry VI* which, according to the estimates of modern critics, were produced in 1592, and treat with scant consideration the question of what magnet drew him to the sources wherein he found the material for his work? Moreover, who among the critics has speculated about the matter of when these plays first took shape in his mind? How long did it take him to read, study, and write dramas of such length? For the date set down for their production is not necessarily the year in which he wrote them.

The problem is complicated by the inclusion of *Two Gentlemen of Verona* in the same year. Four plays of great length within a twelvemonth! Who, before or since, has accomplished such a feat?

I imagine there was a long period of incubation, particularly with regard to the three parts of *Henry VI*, and that he

[9] Regarding dates, see *supra* p. 11, *n*. 5.

had a flair for this study, which came to him when he was a youth. It is my opinion that, in the "lost years," Shakespeare searched industriously all the books that came to his hand for the material of his historical dramas. That leads us to the belief he was at work where there were libraries, and that he was employed by some nobleman who had a company of players, for the hand of a stage craftsman is most noticeable in the work. Notwithstanding the length of the acts, and the many changes of scenes, there is not one that is not shaped for the stage of that day.

This keen desire to use the history of English kings must have been born in him and was fostered during his boyhood. There is no other way to account for the unusual performance of the poet; no other way to explain the industry it would demand.

One of the critics who has pointed directly to Shakespeare's keen interest in the affairs of the life of his time is Dover Wilson. In *The Essential Shakespeare,* he says:

> . . . . We may look for him at the very heart of that life, and picture his eager spirit following the doings of Essex and Raleigh, of Drake and Roger Williams, of Francis Bacon and Robert Cecil, with the keenest possible interest. Not "his tragic life-story," of which we know nothing, but the life at the courts of Elizabeth and James, the persons and doings of the great men of the land, the political and social events of the hour—these form the real background of his plays.[10]

True enough, but this does not tell us how he gathered the information of which he was possessed when he reached London. The famous personages mentioned by Wilson were known to everybody who had eyes and ears. Our poet, however, stripped them naked and knew what they were capable of doing. There was not a twist of their evil desires that he had not studied. "Their virtues else, be they as pure as

[10] Cambridge University Press, 1948, pp. 12-3.

grace, as infinite as man may undergo, shall in the general censure take corruption from that particular fault." [11] *Foul play!*

The plays reveal a knowledge of men and their iniquities that goes much farther back than the reign of Elizabeth. War, religious strife, depopulation, the severities of the acts against vagabondage, harlotry, the gossip of the inns, the troubles of carters—there's no end to it; he knew the life of them all, inside and out, stripped to their very vitals. From the scholars we get little to explain passage after passage in comedy and tragedy, or to enlighten us about life as he saw it. There seems to me no reason why the critics should pass so lightly over the bitter outpouring of his mind. Others have expressed themselves as forcibly upon man and his activities.

He was not content to deal with a slice of life. His insatiable appetite craved knowledge of the whole of it. All were to him part and parcel of existence, as it was lived by high and low, rich and poor, polite and vulgar, guilty and innocent. As Goethe would say, "Man, himself—not mankind!"

It was Blaise Pascal, fifty or sixty years later, who took the full measure of the creature:

> What a chimera then is man! What a novelty! What a monster, what a chaos, what a contradiction, what a prodigy! Judge of all things, imbecile worm of the earth; depositary of truth, a sink of uncertainty and error; the pride and refuse of the universe! [12]

This describes Shakespeare's man.

It would be well for the reader to bear these matters in mind, for when we consider *The Tempest*, they will be valuable aids to our understanding of that play—the valedic-

[11] *Hamlet*, Act I, scene 4.
[12] *Pensées* (Modern Library ed., 1941), p. 143.

tion of a storm-tossed mind, a soul distraught, seeking balm for the spirit before the end.

The themes of these plays are seldom those used by poets. Of course, it may be said that Marlowe and others, notably Kyd in the *Spanish Tragedy*, dealt with blood-and-thunder plots, which drew audiences whose appetites craved such fare. But no poet devoted so much time and work as Shakespeare did to the study of the Plantagenet and Tudor dynasties.

Four

SOCIAL AND
CONSTITUTIONAL
UPHEAVAL

THERE ARE MANY passages in *Henry VI* which indicate clearly what Shakespeare thought of it all. These have not been given due consideration by those investigators who would fathom the poet's soul, and discover what prompted him to expend so many years upon this study. Even Reese, in his long chapter on "Shakespeare's Mind," seems to miss the secret embedded in the poet's brain. He portrays a very different situation from that described in the *Chronicles* of Holinshed and Halle.

It is from this point we begin the exploration of what lay behind the creation of such a figure as Prospero. Perhaps I am mistaken, but I cannot ignore the evidence in *Henry VI* that Shakespeare's whole soul revolted at the royal atrocities of the age.

There are so many instances in this play of what he thought of it that it would take a long essay to deal with them all. In *Henry VI, Part III* we find the King alone, removed from the field of battle. He says:

> Here on this molehill will I sit me down.
> To whom God will, there be the victory!
> For Margaret my queen, and Clifford too,
> Have chid me from the battle; swearing both
> They prosper best of all when I am thence,

Would I were dead! if God's good will were so;
For what is in this world but grief and woe?
O God! methinks it were a happy life,
To be no better than a homely swain;
To sit upon a hill, as I do now,
To carve out dials quaintly, point by point,
Thereby to see the minutes how they run,
How many make the hour full complete;
How many hours bring about the day;
How many days will finish up the year;
How many years a mortal man may live.[1]

This speech came from the soul of a poet. Even a monarch
as blameless as Henry VI—no matter how weary of the
splendors of a throne, nor how earnestly he desired a quiet
life—could not give thought to a contrast so vivid as that it
bears. But more of this. There comes a father with the body
of his son whom he has killed, and Henry hears him cry:

O! pity, God, this miserable age.
What stratagems, how fell, how butcherly,
Erroneous, mutinous, and unnatural,
This deadly quarrel daily doth beget![2]

The King, distraught, cries:

O! pity, pity; gentle heaven, pity.
The red rose and the white are on his face,
The fatal colours of our striving houses:
The one his purple blood right well resembles;
The other his pale cheeks, methinks, presenteth:
Wither one rose, and let the other flourish!
If you contend, a thousand lives must wither.[3]

Foul play is the subject of the histories Shakespeare has
dramatized. The theme runs like the main thread through
the tapestry in which he has woven the fate of kings. The
desire to expose, in plays patronized by high and low, the

[1] Act II, scene 5.
[2] *Ibid.*
[3] *Ibid.*

futility of the schemes and plots to gain regal power, is
evident in all the work that came from his hand. Indeed, we
may search the writings of the dramatists of Greece and
Rome—Aeschylus and Sophocles, Terence and Seneca—
but in none shall we find the lament of a monarch as piteous
as this:

> Gives not the hawthorn bush a sweeter shade
> To shepherds, looking on their silly sheep,
> Than doth a rich embroider'd canopy
> To kings, that fear their subjects' treachery?
> O, yes! it doth; a thousand-fold it doth.
> And to conclude, the shepherd's homely curds,
> His cold thin drink out of his leather bottle,
> His wonted sleep under a fresh tree's shade,
> All which secure and sweetly he enjoys,
> Is far beyond a prince's delicates,
> His viands sparkling in a golden cup,
> His body couched in a curious bed,
> When care, mistrust, and treason wait on him.[4]

Where could such ideas spring from but the mind of one
who had seen the shepherds and their silly sheep?

There are long passages in the plays that appeared after
the death of Elizabeth, which lead one to think that Shakespeare had a keen desire to unburden himself concerning the
fate of Henry VIII's queens. The faked charges brought
against Anne Boleyn and Catherine Howard were not unlike those Leontes brought against Hermione. It is possible
to read the second scene of the third act and feel it was the
fate of the beheaded queens which inspired him to write
The Winter's Tale. Now that the son of Mary, Queen of
Scots, had succeeded Elizabeth, there was no grave reason
why Shakespeare should not write what he was thinking.
James could have had no love for the woman who cut off
his mother's head. He was a Stuart; Elizabeth was a Tudor.

[4] *Ibid.*

For Shakespeare, the last days of the Virgin Queen were filled with troubles that would have tried the soul of a saint. What he endured after the insurrection of Essex and his arrest with Southampton must have been painful in the extreme, and it did not lessen the anguish he felt that Southampton's head remained on his body because of his youth. How many other friends of his were implicated in that reckless adventure? We know more about the matter than some of the critics did a generation ago. It is possible now for the ordinary student to turn to accounts of that disastrous period, which were unknown to or ignored by some of our historians, as well as by those writers on Shakespeare and his times who are in doubt about the facts for and against the conspirators. It is a wonder that Shakespeare controlled his rage and restrained his pen.

Those who imagine *Hamlet* was inspired by the life and fate of Essex overlook the fact that there was only a twelvemonth between the date of the execution of Essex and the appearance of *Hamlet*. The modern critics give 1602 for its production. But in that year they include *All's Well That Ends Well* and *Troilus and Cressida*. If there be one play of Shakespeare which indicates in every scene that it was of slow, deliberate growth, it is *Hamlet*. For anyone to imagine that masterpiece of drama, philosophy, and poetry could have been written in between the intervals of writing the other two seems to me to be carrying genius far beyond its tether. Surely Hamlet, the student-philosopher, wearied of existence, the thought of suicide in his mind, is so utterly unlike the character of Essex that one wonders if some of our Shakespearian scholars have actually compared the two.

The events that occur when we are young remain with us, for they are often discussed by our parents and neighbors. That the mind of a child is something of a *tabula rasa* has been recognized by some of our wisest counsellors. It is a very ancient idea. In the *Timaeus*, Plato says:

> . . . . Truly, as is often said, the lessons which we have learned as children make a wonderful impression on our memories, for I am not sure that I could remember all that I heard yesterday, but I should be much surprised if I forgot any of these things which I have heard very long ago. . . . .[5]

In my own childhood, I remember vividly my father and mother speaking about the Tay Bridge disaster; the loss of the *Eurydice*, the training ship; the Wainwright murder; the laying of the Atlantic cable by the *Great Eastern*. All these extraordinary events were inscribed upon my mind.

Because there were no radios or television sets when Shakespeare was a boy at Stratford, people did not waste their thought upon one-day wonders. Their stock of events was experienced by all and sundry, and these happenings were matters of daily concern to them.

Is it not reasonable to suggest that Shakespeare's grandfather, who was born about the beginning of the sixteenth century, would tell his son the story of the Golden Age, as it was called, when a person could earn enough in thirteen weeks to keep himself and family in food for a year? At that time, beer was a halfpenny the gallon. Although the laborer usually received fourpence a day, the purchasing power of his money has never been exceeded. Beef and mutton were a farthing a pound, and an old song of the time has it: "A bushel of the best wheat cost fourteen pence."

In the *Percy Ballads* a verse confirms this:

I'll tell thee what, good fellow!
Before the friars went hence,

---

[5] *The Works of Plato*, trans. by B. Jowett (N.Y.: Tudor Publishing Co., n.d.), IV, Pt. II, 371-2.

> A bushel of the best wheat
> Was sold for fourteen pence;
> And forty eggs a penny,
> That were both good and new.[6]

It was in the sixteenth century that the warden of Merton College, with some companions and four servants, journeyed on horseback from Oxford to Newcastle. They have left a bill of charges for one day at an inn. The expense amounted to one shilling and a penny for food for seven men. That was indeed the Golden Age for the English laborer, but this condition did not last long, for an Act of Parliament of the time tells us about "greedy and covetous people who accumulate in their hands such great portions of the lands of the realm from the occupying of the poor husbandman, because of the great profit that cometh from sheep."

In 1534 an Act of Parliament dealt with "the wilful waste of houses within this realm and laying to pasture lands which customably had been used for tillage." Another act laid it down that "whosoever decayeth any town, hamlet or house of husbandrie, or shall convert tillage into pasturage, shall forfeit half the profits thereof until the offence be removed."

Such were the stories that John Shakespeare would hear from his father, who would recall the so-called Golden Age, and the vast changes that took place within his lifetime. These would surely be imparted on many occasions, as the times grew harder, and be imprinted upon the minds of the children who gathered about the fireside.

Of this we learn little from the Shakespearian experts, and yet the documentary information of the condition of England is easily found in the records; not only in Acts of Parliament, but in the petitions which came to London from many of the provincial towns. Likewise, the ballads and

[6] As quoted in J. E. Thorold Rogers, *op. cit.*, p. 427.

pamphlets of the time supply much evidence of grave distress.

All this is reflected in many of Shakespeare's plays, and later on I shall quote passages which indicate clearly that he was conscious of the conditions in town and country. It was during the lifetime of Shakespeare's father that Bernard Gilpin, the Bishop of Durham, preached a sermon before Edward VI. Here are some of the passages that describe the state of the poor, as he knew it:

> Be the poor man's cause never so manifest, the rich shall for money find six or seven Councillors that shall stand with subtleties and sophisms to cloak an evil matter and hide a known truth. Such boldness have the covetous cormorants that now their robberies, extortion and open oppression, have no end or limits. . . . . As for turning poor men out of their holdings, they take it for no offence, but say their land is their own, and they turn them out of their shrouds like mice. Thousands in England, through such, beg now from door to door, which once kept honest houses. . . . . Poor men are daily hunted out of their livings, there is no covert or den can keep them safe. . . . .[7]

It is hard to account for the silence of the scholars about this aspect of affairs. Why they should ignore the records of the iniquities which arose in the reign of Henry VIII cannot be explained.

Moreover, it is difficult to understand why our historians of polite literature are desirous of steering clear of the documented story of the real conditions of the Tudor period. The excuse of lack of evidence cannot be made, for in well-stocked libraries many works may be found, written during the reign of Elizabeth and James I, which give a fairly clear picture of the woeful state into which the people of England had fallen. Here are some lines from a ballad:

[7] Delivered in 1552.

> Commons to close and keep
> Poor folk for bread to cry and weep;
> Towns pulled down to pasture sheep,
> This is the new guise.[8]

The English religious and social reformer, Robert Crowley, who lived in the sixteenth century, wrote:

> Lord God! (quod this marchaunt)
>   in Turkey have I been,
> Yet among those heathen
>   none such cruelty have I seen.[9]

Perhaps the keenest critic of the time was Thomas Dekker, the fellow-playwright of Shakespeare. In his work, *The Belman of London,* he describes vividly the condition of the country as he saw it:

> I began to hate it worse than before I loved it; I fell to dispraise it faster than ever I did commend it. For I found it full of care, and full of craft; full of labor and yet full of penury. I saw the poor husbandman made a slave to the rich farmer, the farmer racked by his landlord. I saw that covetousness made dear years when she had fullest barns, and to curse plenty for being liberal of her blessings.[10]

Phillip Stubbes, who lived at the time of Shakespeare, wrote in *The Anatomy of Abuses in England:*

> God give them grace to lay open their enclosures again, to let fall their rents, fines, incomes, and other impositions whereby God is offended, the poor breth-

---

[8] This will be found in *Ballads from MSS.*, ed. by Frederick J. Furnivall, 1868-72, I, 97. For an interesting "devaluation of the Elizabethan Age" see Oscar Sherwin's two articles, "All That Glisters is not Gold," *Amer. Journ. Econ. & Socio.*, VI (April, 1947), 387-401 and (July, 1947), 549-60.

[9] *The Way to Wealth* (London, 1872), p. 132.

[10] *The Non-Dramatic Works of Thomas Dekker*, 5 vols. (London: Grosart, 1884), III, 111-2.

ren beggared, and I fear me, the whole realm will be brought to utter ruin and decay.[11]

From such evidence we might conclude that foul play was the order of the day.

I can well understand how the ordinary readers, who merely "go through" Shakespeare's plays, may miss the points I am making. Most of them have no background that would enable them to grasp many subtle references to the condition of affairs. However, it is quite different with the Shakespearian scholars. Perhaps they are so taken up with the problems of authorship of the texts, and the sources of the plays, that they have not thought it worth while to go deeply into the matter of Shakespeare's attitude to the lamentable changes which had taken place under the Tudors.

Another matter of importance that should be considered in this respect is the natural inclination to regard the Elizabethan period through modern eyes. The polite society in which the critic moves today did not exist then. There were many Calibans on the loose in "civilized" England itself, and greed and crime were rife. Bloodshed was a pastime, and often before the hanging or the execution, additional torture would be applied.

The blood-and-thunder plays of the dramatists of the period were relished by the rich as lustily as by the poor. But Tyburn was the real show. There, the actual thing was presented; no make-believe of actors of the Globe. There were galleries and boxes at Marble Arch, and the gallows was the stage. Seats fetched high prices, and it is recorded that many of the patrons protested because they could not find a good place from which to see the horror.

In some of the old documents there are vivid descriptions of the proceedings, when a condemned person was taken to Tyburn to be hanged. Here is one of 1499 that is typical,

[11] Reprint (London: New Shakespeare Society, 1877-79), Pt. I, sec. 6, p. 117.

written in the English of the period, but I shall put it into modern language. It concerns the fate of Perkin Warbeck and the Earl of Warwick. The trial took place at Westminster. Twelve men were accused: "There they all were attainted, and judgment given that they should be drawn on hurdles from the Tower, throughout London, to the Tyburn, and there to be hanged, and cut down quick, and their bowels to be taken out and burned; their heads to be stricken off and quartered, their heads and quarters to be disposed at the King's pleasure." [12]

This was the fate of Perkin and his fellow conspirators. The Earl of Warwick, however, was beheaded on Tower Hill.

Should any student wish more information about the methods of dealing with criminals, real or supposed, he cannot do better than consult the bibliography in Dr. Margaret Murray's extraordinary book, *The Divine King in England*. The list runs to more than two hundred sources, most of which are the documents of the period.

It is hard to explain why some critics should be shocked at the vulgarity and bawdy speech of Shakespeare's men and women of the "lower classes," and yet overlook the atrocities of Tower Hill and Tyburn. Dr. Murray's work is a revelation of what took place in the lifetime of Richard Shakespeare, his son, and his grandson, and it supplies facts that are new to our students of the Tudor period. Historically the book is indispensable, and, as a picture of the times, it gives us a better comprehension of the direful events that were known to Shakespeare, and saddened many a day for him.

[12] See Margaret Murray, *op. cit.*, p. 124.

Five

THE "LOST YEARS"

LET US NOW speculate about the period of Shakespeare's life before he married in 1582, which has been called the "lost years," and is usually ignored by the critics for lack of data. The official records are silent between the date of his christening and his eighteenth year, but we may safely assume that his primary schooling was finished some four years before his marriage. The boys of that time entered universities at a much earlier age than they do now. It was a far easier matter to school them then, for the curriculum was not cluttered up with a thousand and one subjects that seriously handicap the education of the modern boy.

At St. Paul's in London, where John Colet was dean (1505-19), the choirboys were taught the essentials of learning, and Latin, of course, was one of the chief subjects. As early as Alfred's day, "Boys not only read Virgil, but they were encouraged to write Latin verses themselves." [1] At Eton, Westminster, and other colleges, the boys acted in Latin plays, and F. E. Halliday tells us in his work, *Shakespeare and His Critics:*

> The importance that was attached to acting may be gauged from the fact that in 1546 students of Queen's College, Cambridge, who failed to take part in a play

[1] R. H. Hodgkin, *A History of the Anglo-Saxons*, 2 vols. (2nd ed.; Oxford University Press, 1939), II, 437.

or to attend a performance once a year were liable to be sent down.[2]

Whether such a system was in vogue at the grammar school in Stratford I doubt, but we may be sure that the boys were drilled in Latin from an early age. In this connection, we must remember that Cranmer's reformed liturgy bore the date of 1549, about twenty-five years before Shakespeare became a student.

There would be many people in Stratford who had attended Catholic services when they were boys, and even if they became Protestants later, they would remember the Latin Mass, and use many phrases in Latin when they were in a religious mood. What I wish to establish here is that it was no strange tongue when Shakespeare was a boy.

Between the time he left school and married Anne, there might have been many opportunities for him to become associated with bands of strolling players or, indeed, with the noble companies that played at Kenilworth and other great houses in and about Warwickshire. We do know that he was a handsome lad, and I think it quite probable that he was cast for many a girl's part. If the reports of his physical appearance may be accepted, he undoubtedly would have made a charming heroine in the plays then acted. Add to this a knowledge of music and a melodious voice, and he would have been an acquisition to any company.

From my own experience (and I draw upon that in working this problem out), I know thoroughly well the inclinations of young people who are stage struck. A zealous pupil in a stock company is not satisfied merely to play a part, but is eager at all times to learn everything that can be known about the production of a play. In my own case, I produced seventeen plays within five years, which was considered a most unusual achievement. This did not include the work I did at the Royal Opera at Covent Garden. I mention this

[2] London: Gerald Duckworth & Co., 1950, p. 76.

solely for the purpose of illustrating what the stage-struck young man or woman is capable of accomplishing.

One thing in connection with Shakespeare that should not be overlooked is his experience with re-hashing old plays (to use the stage expression). It is purely and simply hack work, but it is the best method I know for learning the technique of writing and producing one. We can well imagine Shakespeare engaged in this occupation during those years before he married Anne.

Another question occurs: At what period of his career did he come in contact with the motley customers of the taverns? Where did he meet Mistress Quickly, Pistol, Bardolph, and Nym? It might be said they were among the strolling players who visited Stratford. Yes, that is likely enough; but he took more than a glimpse of them, and the players visited his town only at odd intervals. My feeling is that he must have been associated with them, traveled with them, for they were likely to be the hangers-on of companies that visited the town. It requires no stretch of the imagination to contemplate the scum and dross of wars, and other piracies, tagging at the heels of strolling players, for there would be high festival when they gave their plays; plenty to eat and drink, pockets to pick, and other nefarious bits of business to which outcasts resort.

There must have been a period, before he married Anne, when he joined some strolling players of the meanest order, who presented their plays in the small towns on market days. There are records among the antiquities of the shires, particularly Warwickshire and Shropshire, which give the dates when markets were held, and it is surprising to find that many of the places were busier centers in the sixteenth century than they were in the nineteenth, probably because the capitals and larger towns offered greater opportunities to producers.

Shakespeare's "lost years" fall into two periods: 1578-82

and 1585-92. The first covers the years between the time when he left grammar school—at the age of fourteen, perhaps—and when he had intercourse with Anne. His eldest child, Susanna, was christened on May 26, 1583. The special license for his marriage is dated November 27, 1582, so we may imagine that he was in Stratford—or Shottery, a mile away, where Anne lived—in the summer of that year. The twins, Hamnet and Judeth, were christened on February 2, 1585. There is no record of children other than these.

The second period of the "lost years" extends for seven years—or perhaps more—from 1585 to 1592. It is in these two periods that he must have served his apprenticeship as a player and as a student. Moreover, there probably were close at hand works which he read, to fit himself for writing his earliest plays. The Latin authors must have attracted him from the beginning, and perhaps he was especially drawn to the tragedies of Seneca.

The first period of the "lost years" gave him the chance to meet the motley crowd he pictures so sharply in *Henry IV* and *Henry V*. Pistol, Bardolph, Nym, Poins and the Boy are no creatures of the imagination. They were seen; indeed, the observer probably rubbed elbows with them; they must have "sat" for him, for they are etched as clearly as Dürer himself could present them. Each one is different in speech, in gait and appearance. The Boy's description of Bardolph's nose; Nym's "That's the humor of it"; Pistol's oaths and braggadocio; these single them out as peculiar specimens of the bawdy taverns. Another clue to them and their activities is the classical quotations some of them picked up from the pieces given by the strolling players. They would mouth the speeches they heard and be as keen about the acting as Mistress Quickly herself.

I take it that the Boy in *Henry V* was the one that Prince Hal gave to Falstaff. Sir John having passed away, he was taken into the service of Nym, Pistol and Bardolph. They have followed Henry to France and, after Fluellen comes upon them loafing, and drives them up to the breach, the Boy is left alone and sums them up thus:

> As young as I am, I have observed these three swash-ers. I am boy to them all three, but all they three, though they would serve me, could not be man to me; for, indeed three such antiques do not amount to a man. For Bardolph, he is white-livered and red-faced; by the means whereof, a' faces it out, but fights not. For Pistol, he hath a killing tongue and a quiet sword; by the mean whereof a' breaks words and keeps whole weapons. For Nym, he hath heard that men of few words are the best men; and therefore he scorns to say his prayers, lest a' should be thought a coward: but his few bad words are matched with as few good deeds; for a' never broke any man's head but his own, and that was against a post when he was drunk. They will steal any thing and call it purchase. Bardolph stole a lute-case, bore it twelve leagues, and sold it for three half-pence. Nym and Bardolph are sworn brothers in filching, and in Calais they stole a fire-shovel; I knew by that piece of service the men would carry coals,—they would have me as familiar with men's pockets as their gloves or their handkerchers: which makes much against my manhood if I should take from another's pocket to put into mine; for it is plain pocketing up of wrongs. I must leave them and seek some better service: their villany goes against my weak stomach, and there I must cast it up.[3]

This speech bears all the marks of having been heard by the dramatist. Perhaps Shakespeare was the boy who had to "seek some better service." Anyway, it is the verdict of the pot-boy, the stirrup-holder, the jordan-emptier, a living creature cast for the role of serving menials.

This is only a conjecture as to what might have taken place during his apprenticeship, before the banns were issued for his marriage, but perhaps it is as good as any other. For,

[3] Act III, scene 2.

if we are to understand how it was that Shakespeare began his career in London, with plays of such varied subject matter as low comedy and melodrama, we must account for an intensive apprenticeship and the zeal to become a capable dramatist. I submit that Shakespeare's so-called "lost years" (before his marriage), which so many of the critics are afraid to account for, are those in which he was traveling about the country as a player of women's parts, as a singer, and as a hack, supplying new garbs for old pieces.

The second obscure period of "lost years" must have been the time when he gathered the material for his plays. What could such a genius accomplish in this direction during six or eight years? The histories alone must have required unending hours of labor to gather facts for the plots and counter-plots of these stories. When we think of the time he must have spent in reading about the pre-Tudor dynasties, we are at a loss to estimate what a day's work meant to him. Perhaps he was one of those singular geniuses who absorbs books. George Douglas Brown, when discussing Shakespeare, often used to say he knew how to "pluck the guts" out of a tome.

Furthermore, we are amazed at the speed with which he composed. His ideas gushed forth like torrents from spring freshets. The broken line bears witness to the haste with which he wrote. These gaps had to be left unfinished, for the idea urged him on toward full expression, lest it should vanish while he paused to attend to form and complete the line. It is not difficult to realize that he never found time to take up a play again and fill in the gaps, for he must have gone on to another immediately, perhaps even while rehearsing the one just written. Who but a journeyman-genius of the stage could perform such wonders?

The perfect technique of his craft is stamped on nearly every scene he wrote. But this can be appreciated only by the man of the theater, who reads the play with a view to producing it. The deftness of his characterization is unsurpassed. His men and women speak a language which is their own. Very rarely does one indulge in the glorious bombast of Tamburlaine. Shakespeare's educated men and women refer to classical figures and scenes they learned to know when they were scholars. The common folk speak the idiom to which they were born.

Herein lies the difference between Shakespeare and Marlowe, whose Scythian shepherd knew as much about the classics as a university don. Indeed, it might be said that Marlowe, the poet, is Tamburlaine, and never saw a sheep or a goat anywhere near Samarkand. Yet, it must be admitted the play was a great success. But this fact, which is well attested, makes us wonder how an audience which welcomed *Tamburlaine* could, within three or four years, as readily accept *Love's Labour's Lost* and *Henry VI*.

Here, let us spend a moment upon the wide differences between the methods of Shakespeare and Marlowe, because there should be no doubt in the reader's mind about the authorship of Shakespeare's plays. We may ask ourselves if there is anything in Marlowe's work that indicates he could have written *As You Like It, Twelfth Night* or *The Winter's Tale*. I shall go so far as to say that nowhere does Marlowe show that he had the mind equipped for writing the tragedies.

The splendor of the verse of *Tamburlaine* and the other pieces thrills us—indeed, keys us up to such a pitch of admiration that we lose all sense of characterization. We do not stop to ask whether a Scythian shepherd would be familiar with the classics, although the original one (Timūr) read the Koran. Would Shakespeare be guilty of such a literary indiscretion as to give to an unlearned person such phrases as "the eldest son of heavenly Ops" or "mighty Jove"? Surely it is stretching the poetic bow to its utmost strength when a Scythian shepherd speaks about "Clymene's brainsick son." But these indiscretions are carried *ad absur-dum* when Tamburlaine talks about "Plato's wondrous year."

Nevertheless, the tragedy is a poetic masterpiece, no matter what classical references are scattered through the speeches of Tamburlaine. Dramatically, it is a gorgeous pageant.

In workmanship, in characterization, these two poets are poles apart. Shakespeare's plays were written for the stage, a fact which erudite literary critics are wont to overlook. He could have had no more idea that they would be used for any other purpose than he could have imagined the clergymen of the time taking texts from Venus and Adonis for their sermons.

The plays were performed before they were published, and so little was Shakespeare interested in this form of expression that it is doubtful if he ever saw the page proofs of one of them. The library and the stage are two entirely different spheres of thought and action.

During the twelve or fifteen years of my active work in the theater, I must have read between three and four hundred plays for my employers. Not a few were literal translations from French and German successes. Some were from the poets of that period; others from well-known playwrights; most of them from budding novelists. It was my office to separate those that might be accepted for rehearsal from those I thought had no chance of attracting an audience who would pay for production. Out of that total I remember only six that achieved any success.

For the man of the theater, it is solely a question of what will act. This fact was so well understood in my day that some actor-managers would not permit an author to read a play aloud, lest he give dramatic effect to it. The story may be apocryphal, but it is told that one actor-manager (I have forgotten whether it was Tree or George Alexander) was so taken by someone reading a play that he snatched the manuscript from the author after the first act, saying, "It sounds too good; I'll have to read it myself."

In conclusion, then, let us keep in mind constantly the difference that lies between the approach of a literary expert to the plays and the method of a producer who has to present the piece.

Six

SHAKESPEARE'S APPRENTICESHIP

ALAN KEEN's discovery of Halle's *Chronicle* (issue of 1550), with the marginal notes in a Shakespearian hand,[1] has thrown new light on the "lost years." It is now possible to piece together a plausible story of where Shakespeare spent that time, or part of it, and by whom he was employed. The volume examined by Keen was at one time in the possession of Sir Richard Newport of High Ercall, in Shropshire, who died in 1570.

The author of this chronicle, *The Union of the Noble and Illustre Famelies of Lancastre and York*, was a Shropshire man himself, born at Northall about 1498. The work was first published in 1542, and most of the critics consider it the prime source of the historical plays.

With these few clues we are led to speculate about young William's reason for leaving Stratford. Alan Keen suggests that it concerned the faith of his father, John Shakespeare. According to the records, he did not attend church service, and it was thought by his neighbors that he was a recusant. Perhaps John sent William away because of the sectarian bitterness that was rife in Warwickshire. Some of the critics hold that the Shakespeares never changed their faith. Others are firm in the belief that William was a Protestant. Evidence

[1] *The Annotator, cit. supra.*

of this latter point of view is set forward in Marchette Chute's book, *Shakespeare of London:*

> . . . . When the Walker family of Stratford named their son William, Shakespeare acted as godfather at the baptism, and he could not have done so unless he were an accredited member of the Church of England.[2]

Such proof of a change of faith scarcely takes into consideration the terrors of the time. The new Protestantism was only about six years old when Shakespeare was born, and under Mary, much of the work of her father was undone. Hooper, the Bishop of Gloucester, was burned in his own cathedral city, and Ferrar, the Bishop of St. David's, had suffered a similar fate at Caermarthen. Latimer and Ridley perished in the pyre at Oxford. Even Cranmer, the Archbishop, met a similar fate. Before he was put to the flames, he recanted in the Church of St. Mary at Oxford, and said:

> Now I come to the great thing that troubleth my conscience more than any other thing that ever I said or did in my life, and that is the setting abroad of writings contrary to the truth; which here I now renounce and refuse as things written by my hand contrary to the truth which I thought in my heart, and written for fear of death to save my life, if it might be.[3]

There must have been thousands in the England of Mary, who changed about from one creed to another, in the hope of saving their lives. Protestantism was of very slow growth, so far as the mass of the people was concerned. What did they know about theological differences and a newer ritual? The record shows plainly that the religious strife was carried on for years during the reign of Elizabeth. And Shake-

[2] N.Y.: E. P. Dutton, 1949, p. 10.
[3] As quoted in Green, *A Short History* . . . . , p. 367.

speare, in one of his later plays, which appeared in 1602, remarks:

> . . . . If men could be contented to be what they are, there were no fear in marriage; for young Charbon the puritan, and old Poysam the papist, howsome'er their hearts are severed in religion, their heads are both one; they may joul horns together like any deer i' the herd.[4]

Take good notice that it is a clown who utters this. In passing, I may remark that in many of the plays Shakespeare's own mind is expressed by the fellow who wears motley.

Some of the critics who think Shakespeare was a Catholic base their notion upon the story that his father was accused of being a recusant. Whether he was or not is not clear. However, we have the evidence that the service at Holy Trinity, when he was buried, was a Protestant one.

Dover Wilson asks, "Is *The Tempest* a Christian play?" And he replies to his own question:

> . . . . It is surely a profoundly religious poem, and of a Christ-like spirit in its infinite tenderness, its all-embracing sense of pity, its conclusion of joyful atonement and forgiveness, so general that even Caliban begins to talk of "grace." But it is not in the least Christian from the theological standpoint; there is no word of God, not a hint of immortality. . . . .[5]

On the other hand, Robert Speaight's essay, *Nature in Shakespearian Tragedy*,[6] treats the play as a highly moral work, pointing to the salvation of sinners through grace. Yet, he warns the reader:

> It is one thing to hesitate before stating, as a matter of proven fact, that Shakespeare held this or that

[4] *All's Well That Ends Well*, Act I, scene 3.
[5] *Op. cit.*, p. 144.
[6] London: Hollis & Carter, 1955.

personal belief; the sum of contemporary beliefs com-
pose the spiritual matter of his *oeuvre*. But it is folly to
imagine that he can be properly understood without
reference to the theological commonplaces—or novel-
ties—of his time. . . . .[7]

I do not see what is to be gained by entering into these
deeply controversial problems. Shakespeare was not a bishop
or a lay-preacher. He was an actor-dramatist—a man of the
theater. So far as the church and the educated laity were
concerned, the player was something of an outcast. As for
the authorities questioning an actor about his religious beliefs, the idea seems too preposterous for consideration. I do
not think anyone of influence would give a second thought
to such a notion.

There is no record of one turning "hot-gospeler," going
about proselytizing for one sect or another. Why should an
actor of that day risk his living—perhaps his life—by declar-
ing himself an adherent of the creed that was not sanctioned
at the moment? Moreover, the stage was not a pulpit, nor
was it an altar. It catered to sinners, no matter what their
beliefs were, and gave them the fare that entertained their
worldly appetites.

Sermons were for the divines to preach—according to
the belief of the day—when they were not splitting hairs
about theology and church reform. Elizabeth herself was
no devout churchgoer, although she attended services as a
matter of course, and understood the ritual. She was all for
religious harmony, no matter what the difficulties were that
harassed Protestants and Catholics.

As for the ecclesiastical authorities of that day, it may be
assumed (owing to their antipathy to the stage) that they
imagined there were no actors in heaven, and the devil
thought they were not worth burning. Players were beyond

[7] P. 165.

the pale—mere puppets, whose purpose was to amuse all and sundry, irrespective of creed and ritual.

I think Shakespeare was a deeply religious man. No one who loved Nature and knew her so well could be otherwise. Nearly a hundred years before our poet was born, Dürer, the great genius of brush and pencil, was at work in Nuremberg, and in his writings we find a statement on Nature that seems to fit Shakespeare: "For in truth art lies hidden in Nature—he who can wrest it from her possesses art." [8]

The idea conveyed in this statement of Dürer can be traced in many of Shakespeare's plays. There are passages in *Hamlet* that could have been written only by a deeply reverent man. The fear of a life after death was ever present in his mind. Not only do we find this spiritual anxiety expressed in his worthy characters; it often appears in the reflections of his villains. The hereafter was an obsession that prompted the poet to pen many a memorable line. I think it is necessary to understand this if we are to fathom the mystery of redemption, as it is given to us in *The Tempest*. We may be sure the play came from the mind of a poet who was conscious of the creative power of God.

Many of the critics agree that fear was always in the mind of Shakespeare. That this was so can be gathered from the plays of the earliest period. But it was not physical, it was spiritual fear. He lived in a time when fear multiplied fear daily. How he escaped from the toils of conspirators and factions of denominationalists is a mystery. But it indicates that he threw his whole soul into his work as a dramatist, and buried within himself those opinions sometimes blurted out by his characters, either in asides, or in the remarks of a clown.

This whole matter of the faith of John Shakespeare is

[8] W. Waetzoldt, *Dürer and His Times* (N.Y.: Phaidon Publishers Inc., 1950), p. 220.

still unsettled by the experts. Although Reese enters thoroughly into the question, he comes to no decision. The matter is left open.

Whether William's father surrendered to Protestantism, under the compulsions of the time, is of no importance in this disquisition, for we are concerned wholly with the occurrences in English life that would be written upon the mind of our poet. The swing of the pendulum, ticking off the years of the religious strife, moved from Catholicism to Protestantism, from Protestantism to Catholicism, and then back to Protestantism. Bloody Mary was no better than her father.

Some of the critics are under the impression that with the coming of Elizabeth to the throne, the Protestant faith was adopted as a matter of course. It is strange that such an idea should be held by anyone who has read the documents and letters of the powerful families in the north of England. We learn from them that the old faith did not die a sudden death on the demise of Mary. The Mass of the Catholics was carried on by secular priests in many a manor. I have been in several that still have their private chapels, although the service is now conducted by Protestant clergymen. At Hatfield, at Llantarnam Abbey and other places, which antedate the coming of Elizabeth, I have visited them.

In this connection, a new translation of the autobiography of an Elizabethan has been published. *William Weston*[9] tells the story of a Jesuit priest who was in England during the reign of the Virgin Queen. He found a patron in the Earl of Arundel. In 1586 he was arrested as one concerned in the Babington plot. After severe cross examination, he was spared the fate of the gallows, but when the Spanish invasion was threatened, the government decided to imprison priests and their Catholic laity in Wisbech castle. Weston suffered great

[9] Trans. from the Latin by Philip Caraman (London: Longmans, Green & Co., 1955).

hardship, but in 1594, he and his fellows were given more lenient treatment, and they organized themselves into a group to debate the burning questions concerning the old and the new faiths. We find that many Catholics attended these conferences, and that some Protestants were converted.

This is only one instance of a priest in England during Elizabeth's reign, who carried on the work of the old faith, and his story indicates that there was no swift change of belief. Many who maintained their services in their private chapels did so in spite of fear of the block or the gallows.

Shakespeare kept his religious beliefs to himself, not because he was afraid of suffering if he declared them, but for a far better reason—they were his, deeply embedded in his own soul, and he was answerable to no one but his Creator.

It may be asked: Through what educative process did he learn the wisdom of avoiding all religious controversy? In one of his earliest plays he puts into the mouth of a king these words:

> . . . . I always thought
> It was both impious and unnatural
> That such immanity and bloody strife
> Should reign among professors of one faith.[10]

It could not be said in plainer terms. Therefore, I have no qualms about the thoughts that molded Shakespeare's mind in the years before he was married, nor have I any doubts about the cultural circle of people with whom he was associated in the second period of the "lost years." For his knowledge could have been gathered only in a great manor house, where there was a collection of books made by a lover of the liberal arts. Such a collection as Prospero had.

For many years I have held the notion that Shakespeare was one of those choristers who did not suffer the usual change in voice. That he was a skilled musician and had the

[10] *I Henry VI*, Act V, scene 1.

most beautiful sense of melody, no one can deny who has enjoyed the lyrics scattered through the plays. Every one lends itself to music.

He lived in the time of William Byrd, when the madrigal was a favorite form of composition. So, if I am correct in this view, he might easily have found a patron who kept players and loved music. Sir Francis Newport, son of Sir Richard, at High Ercall was such a man, and perhaps it was there he found Halle's *Chronicle*.

The earliest plays of Shakespeare clearly indicate to me that the author had at hand for several years what would then be a well-stocked library. He must have been living in a cultural circle where he could devote himself to reading, in preparation for writing the histories, and acquiring the knowledge that is evident in the scenes of *Love's Labour's Lost*, *The Comedy of Errors* and *Two Gentlemen of Verona*.

We may assume no library at Stratford would contain the volumes he must have read at that stage of his career. His love of books is expressed in play after play, and his knowledge of witches, covens, Salic law, and other unusual subjects goes far to convince me that his later studies were pursued in the library of a patron of high degree.

The more I think of the amazing output of plays written by Shakespeare in the first eight years of his career—say from 1588 to 1596—the more certain I become that he had far greater advantages for study than fell to the lot of an ordinary strolling player of that day. A glance at the historical order of the plays, as determined by modern critics, should convince anyone who has read them that the author had a well-informed mind. The variety of subjects is extraordinary. Think of the writer of *Love's Labour's Lost* turning to such a history as *Richard III*. It is hard to imagine any poet who has attempted drama since his time treating of two such entirely different subjects as *Titus Andronicus* and

Romeo and Juliet. Other wide differences could easily be shown between plays written within the same decade.

Where, then, we ask, did he find his subjects? The critics have given many of the sources of his work. But where, before he reached London, could he seek a library containing these works? There were no secondhand bookstalls in that day; no free lending libraries; and it does not seem likely that he picked them up, one by one, as he roamed through the country. The most reasonable conclusion we can reach about this phase is that he was employed by a man who was a lover of books. And when one considers the sources of his work, and the learning that is put into them, we should feel sure that he had a patron who helped him in every way to use his library.

There is much more to be considered about the apprenticeship of our author—before he married Anne, and after—than we find in the essays of the scholars. Of course, many of their works were written before Alan Keen discovered his copy of Halle's *Chronicle*. That Shakespeare might have found his way to High Ercall is an attractive notion for anyone who is familiar with the counties of the Marsh that borders on Offa's Dyke.

References to Shropshire in the plays convince me that the writer saw what he is describing. I have referred to some of these in my essay, *Hamlet and Shakespeare*. Who but a man who had seen the river and knew it well could speak of the "sandy-bottom'd Severn"? Some of the critics suggest that he spent some time in the Cotswolds. His pictures of scenes that are reminiscent of that district would also fit the country round about High Ercall, for on a clear day one can see the Wrekin and the Ercall, and beyond, the Welsh Hills.

High Ercall is described in Domesday, and in *Antiquities of Shropshire*, the Reverend R. W. Eyton says: "Ercall was the Caput of those vast estates which formed the heritage of the Newports;—a heritage than which none greater has accrued to any single Shropshire family since the advent of the Normans." [11]

If Shakespeare did go to High Ercall, the Newport house in Shropshire, what road would he take? From Stratford he would probably make his way through Alcester to Bridgnorth, and travel along the highway to Tong. In the church there are the tombs of Sir Thomas and Sir Edward Stanley, with poetical epitaphs supposed to have been composed by Shakespeare, according to a manuscript of *c*. 1630. Halliwell-Phillipps reproduces it in facsimile in his Folio of 1853.

From Tong Shakespeare would perhaps pass near Buildwas and Wenlock, where he would see the wreck of those two great monastic houses. The next place of deep interest to him would be Lillieshall. If he were with a band of strolling players, the town of Newport would be the next stop. High Ercall is only a short distance from there. This slight clue is worth while pursuing, for it takes us to a part of England where he would have heard Welsh people pronouncing English.

In *The Merry Wives of Windsor* a Welsh parson, Sir Hugh Evans, is given the pronunciation of our speech that the Welsh used when I was a boy and lived with my grandparents in Shropshire. Evans says:

> It is petter that friends is the sword, and end it; and there is also another device in my prain, which, peradventure, prings goot discretion with it. . . . .[12]

Why should Welsh people go to Warwickshire for a living when Shropshire was near at hand? Indeed, I do not think Shakespeare would find a Welshman in Warwickshire who would express himself as Evans does to Simple, in this same play:

[11] Twelve vols. (London: John Russell Smith, 1859), IX, 62.
[12] Act I, scene 1.

Pless my soul! how full of chollors I am, and trem-
pling of mind! I shall be glad if he have deceived me.
How melancholies I am! I will knog his urinals about
his knave's costard when I have goot opportunities for
the 'ork: pless my soul![13]

I can imagine that acute mind of Shakespeare taking in
the speech of Welsh folk on market days in Shrewsbury,
only a short journey from High Ercall.

Another instance of Welsh pronunciation of English
words will be found in the lines of Fluellen, in *Henry V*.
Surely the following was written by one who had actually
heard the Welsh speak English:

> . . . . The rascally, scald, beggarly, lousy, pragging
> knave, Pistol,—which you and yourself and all the
> 'orld know to be no petter than a fellow,—look you
> now, of no merits, he is come to me and prings me
> pread and salt yesterday, look you, and pid me eat my
> leek. . . . .[14]

In this search for evidence of where Shakespeare spent
his days before he made his appearance in London, there is
no clue so pregnant with possibilities as the one laid down
by Alan Keen since his discovery of the annotated Halle's
Chronicle.

Another link in this story of his whereabouts and occupation during the "lost years" is that which Alan Keen notes
in the will of Alexander Houghton of Lea, Lancashire. This
man died in 1581, and bequeathed to his brother "all my
Instrumentes belonginge to mewsyckes and all maner of
playe clothes yf he be mynded to keppe and doe keppe
playeres." If the brother did not desire to keep players, the
will directed that Sir Thomas Hesketh should have the
instruments, and further:

[13] Act III, scene 1.
[14] Act V, scene 1.

> . . . . I most hertelye requyre the said Sir Thomas to
> be ffrendlye unto ffoke Gyllome and William Shake-
> shafte now dwellynge with me and eyther to take them
> ynto his Servyce or els to helpe theym to some good
> master as my tryste ys he will.[15]

This opens up a further field for speculation. There seem
to have been very close associations among the families of
Lancashire houses, and the lords of the manors were known
to have companies of players and musicians. The Houghtons,
the Heskeths and the Stanleys lived not far apart, and Ruf-
ford Hall is only a few miles from Knowsley. According to
the genealogical tables in *The Annotator*, intermarriage and
other close associations were as frequent there as they were
in Shropshire among the Newports, the Corbets, the Actons
and the Levesons. It is possible, even that after the death of
Sir Richard Newport, his copy of Halle's *Chronicle* was
bequeathed to Sir Thomas Hesketh, whose players might
have visited Shrewsbury or the great houses at Lillieshall or
Morton Corbet.

It seems to me that, if Shakespeare was in the service of
Alexander Houghton, he must have made his way at some
time through Shropshire to the banks of the Mersey. I
should not be surprised to hear that Alan Keen had discovered further documents revealing some precise history of the
journeyings during the "lost years." Perhaps in an old letter
he may find a reference to the wandering of Sir Richard
Newport's annotated copy of Halle's *Chronicle*.

Frequently, in Shakespearian criticism, the question of
plagiarism is raised. To this I reply, "Yes, he was a plagiarist.
But so were all the others of that period." If we are to be
purists on this question, we shall have to go back to the first
of the Greek dramatists; and, for all we know, Aeschylus

---

[15] See Alan Keen's letter in *The Times Literary Supplement*, November 18, 1955, p. 689.

himself turned to dramatic value the myths that were in the mouths of the people.

Who is not a plagiarist in writing for the stage? The office of the playwright is to outdo the fellow who dramatizes a familiar subject. This craft, of course, does not take into consideration many modern productions which are based upon topical matters. But Shakespeare had a completely new literature to comb for plots and characters. He must have known Florio and have been familiar with much of Montaigne. Perhaps he even met Bruno, for he gives to Hamlet a statement of his about the time of the end of man's life.

The works of the pagan writers—Seneca, Virgil and Ovid —were being read by educated people. North's *Plutarch* was rich meat for the poet's mind, and from it he drew the characters and events that thrill us in *Antony and Cleopatra*, *Coriolanus*, *Timon of Athens*, and *Julius Caesar*. He insured the fame of the author of *Parallel Lives* by dramatizing his stories in glowing verse.

So far as I can remember the work of the Elizabethan dramatists, I can think of only two who would escape the charge of plagiarism as it is known today: Ben Jonson and Thomas Dekker. But is it plagiarism, in the true sense of the term, to use the sources of the stories of the plays without giving credit to their authors? Who of that time would escape censure, when the new literature was flooding the bookstalls of London?

Our scholars are very particular about the sources from which Shakespeare drew his plots and characters. As for similarities of poetic expression, we should not forget that verse was raining from the skies, and I suppose the groundlings then were no different than they are today in repeating lines which took their fancy from plays they saw several times.

When I was a boy in Liverpool, I used to hear the people of Great Charlotte Street Market muttering to themselves, in the gallery of the Amphitheatre, lines from *Hamlet, Macbeth*, or *Richard III*, when Barry Sullivan was playing these roles. We have an instance in *Henry V*, when Pistol spouts classical names. He must have heard them when he saw performances at the early playhouses of London.

There can be no doubt about the apprenticeship that Shakespeare served. As I have already remarked, he must have been engaged for a long time as a "re-hash" or "rewrite" man. His earliest plays indicate he must have spent some busy years learning the technique of the day. He leaves no one in doubt about the locale in which a scene takes place, whereas Marlowe scarcely ever mentions it. It is doubtful whether "Kit" thought of the theater when he wrote *Tamburlaine, The Jew of Malta* and *Doctor Faustus*. Strictly speaking, these are not plays for the stage. They are poetic dramas and could be enjoyed without scenery or costumes. Even the properties in *Tamburlaine* are not essential for theatrical effect.

Let there be no doubt that our poet was an individualist, and quite distinct from other writers for the stage of that period. First, he had a practical knowledge of the stage, as a dramatist and a producer. No one has questioned the fact that he was an actor and, with others, a manager of theaters. Secondly, no one of that period, save perhaps Dekker, brought such living pictures of humble people upon the scene. In Shakespeare's plays we learn what their lives are and what trades occupy them.

Thirdly, our poet is distinct in the originality of such memorable creations as Falstaff, Mistress Quickly, Autolycus, Dogberry, Malvolio, Bardolph, Touchstone, Pistol, Caliban; and a variety of clowns such as Lear's Fool, Lavache, Speed and Launce.

One striking difference between Shakespeare and Marlowe is the evidence, in play after play, that Shakespeare's characters had their feet on the ground. Marlowe is at his best when he is astride a comet, gathering gems for his lines from the stars. His verse soars; he bathes it in the brilliancy of the Milky Way, and his lay figures declaim it, no matter where they are, or what they are doing.

Perhaps the most discriminating test of all is this: Marlowe gives us no song for music. He was no more capable of writing the lyrics we find in the last act of *Love's Labour's Lost* than he could have written a Christmas carol.

Marlowe did not have the homely eye that notes the habits of the folk or the intimate feeling of being one with Nature where there were "daisies pied and violets blue," and "merry larks and ploughmen's clocks." I cannot see him near Dick, who "blows his nail," or giving a passing thought to Marion, whose "nose looks red and raw."

Marlowe's knowledge of women was shallow. Neither Katherine nor Abigail in *The Jew of Malta* can be compared with Imogen, Cordelia, Ophelia, Desdemona, and those superb creations in *Coriolanus:* Volumnia and Virgilia.

Hero and Leander is a mighty work—that part of it written by Marlowe. He stormed the heights of Parnassus and rifled the founts of the Muses for their best treasures to adorn his sparkling verse.

We know of two lyrics by the author of *Tamburlaine:* "The Passionate Shepherd" and "I walkt along a streame for purenesse rare." They contain beautiful lines, but not one with lilt for song, nor one that springs from the hearth. They are charming fancies, but aloof from life lived by the folk of the plough and the milk pail.

Seven

THE PERIOD OF GLOOM

THE FLOODGATES of wrath, stemmed for so long, burst open after the passing of Elizabeth. She died in 1603, and the date given for the appearance of *Timon of Athens* is about 1608. While she lived, Shakespeare hid his inmost thoughts. Yet, sometimes there was a leak in the dam, which let out a trickle of opinion about the condition of things; but in nearly all these cases Shakespeare put the words into the mouth of a clown. Only once that I can recall did any other character but the fool give us an inkling as to his thoughts about human creatures and their iniquities.

In the second act of *As You Like It*, Jaques tells the Duke about meeting with Touchstone:

He that a fool doth very wisely hit
Doth very foolishly, although he smart,
Not to seem senseless of the bob: if not,
The wise man's folly is anatomiz'd
Even by the squandering glances of the fool.
Invest me in my motley; give me leave
To speak my mind, and I will through and through
Cleanse the foul body of th' infected world,
If they will patiently receive my medicine.[1]

When *As You Like It* was written, the time was not ripe for him to speak his mind. The date of the play is 1600, a dangerous period for a critic—whether courtier or poet—to

[1] Act II, scene 7.

raise his voice in public. When Shakespeare went to London about 1587, there was an English army in the Netherlands. That was the year of the execution of Mary Stuart. Then came the revolt in Ireland, and in 1601 Essex, the favorite of the Queen, was beheaded. But the bitterest feud of all was that being waged between Catholics and Protestants. The foul world of London was infected with poisonous strife.

Is it to be supposed Shakespeare was so occupied in writing his plays, and rehearsing them, that he remained in ignorance of the social upheaval? He would have been an unusual citizen if his mind were proof against the calamities of the day. It is hard to account for the light treatment our experts have given to these matters. I think that Shakespeare took them all in as material for his characters, and in some cases, as themes of his plays.

They were convincing evidence of a long period of turmoil. The history of the strife, before he was born, he must have heard from his father's lips. He would be told of atrocities perpetrated in the reign of Henry VIII, which would make those of Aaron and Tamora, in *Titus Andronicus*, seem mild. Lavinia was raped and lost her hands and her tongue; but she was not slowly tortured and then dragged to Tyburn to be hanged. The fate suffered by Richard Whyting would be upon every tongue when John Shakespeare was a boy. Whyting was abbot of Glastonbury, and was bound on a hurdle and dragged to Tor Hill nearby, where he was executed. The recorder reported to Thomas Cromwell, viceregent under Henry VIII, that after his death, his body was cut up, "one quarter standeth at Wells, another at Bath, and at Ilchester and Bridgewater the rest. And his head upon the abbey gate at Glaston." [2]

The writer of the article on Glastonbury in *The Encyclopaedia Britannica* says:

[2] As quoted in Brooks Adams, *The Law of Civilization and Decay* (N.Y.: Alfred A. Knopf, 1943), p. 242.

A darker passage does not occur in the annals of the
English Reformation than this murder of an able and
high-spirited man, whose worst offense was that he de-
fended as best he could from the hand of the spoiler the
property in his charge.[3]

Cromwell was no Aaron; he was an educated Englishman,
to whom Henry owed his enormous power as Defender of
the Faith and absolute dictator of the Lords and Commons.

Timon of Athens is such a caldron of vindictive rage and
burning vituperation that some of the critics can justify it
only by suggesting Shakespeare was mad when he wrote it.
Madness is a distemper that is exceedingly difficult to diag-
nose. The fine frenzy of a poet is so unusual, so utterly alien
to the thought of ordinary men, that it can be accounted for
only by considering it as the collapse of a person bereft. The
idea is an ancient one, and we know what Plato thought
about it.

However, in this case, so far as the mind of our poet was
concerned, he must have been quite sober when he wrote this
play. For only a year or two after *Timon* appeared, he wrote
Cymbeline and *The Winter's Tale*, in which we get no evidence of madness. Moreover, *Antony and Cleopatra* and
Coriolanus, both of which bear the imprint of a sane workman, came before Timon. If he were mad when he wrote
Timon, he must have been stricken suddenly and, just as
suddenly, become sane again after the play was finished. For
no one has suggested that either the two plays written before *Timon* or the plays written after it were the productions of a lunatic.

King Lear became mad, but the play was written three
years before *Timon*—about the same time *Macbeth* appeared
—according to the chronological sequence of the plays given
by modern critics. And surely only a poet in full possession
of his faculties could have produced that work.

[3] The article is unsigned (13th ed.), XII, 113.

It is true that Shakespeare himself told us in *A Midsummer Night's Dream:*

The lunatic, the lover, and the poet,
Are of imagination all compact:
One sees more devils than vast hell can hold,
That is, the madman; the lover, all as frantic,
Sees Helen's beauty in a brow of Egypt:
The poet's eye, in a fine frenzy rolling,
Doth glance from heaven to earth, from earth to heaven;
And, as imagination bodies forth
The forms of things unknown, the poet's pen
Turns them to shapes, and gives to airy nothing
A local habitation and a name.[4]

There are three types of madness: the lunatic sees devils; the lover, beauty in a woman's brow; but the poet is quite another person. He "gives to airy nothing a local habitation and a name." This last form of madness has yielded many hours of pure enjoyment for generations of sane men.

It may be that some poets suffer from intermittent lunacy, but not a Shakespeare—not even in such a work as *Timon,* for it reveals creatures who live and move and have their being in every clime under the sun. The wastrel, the syco- phant, the sponger, the ingrate, and the braggart are all familiar figures; but in this play the dramatist deals with the lot, and in its scenes compresses their delinquencies in all their nudity.

If we are to consider a poet mad when "in a fine frenzy rolling," what are we to think of his mental condition when he writes a line that has sanity stamped upon it? Madness, then, must be a momentary affliction, for the lines of most poets do not indicate they are in a fine frenzy rolling from the first to the last one.

Edward Dowden[5] is the one critic who seems to have been

[4] Act V, scene 1.
[5] *Shakspere—A Critical Study of His Mind and Art* (N.Y. and London: Harper & Brothers, 1918; first published 1875; new ed. 1949).

able to interpret correctly the poet's mind during this time, sometimes called "the tragic period." His chapter on "Shakspere's Last Plays" is a revelation, and he completely eschews any notion of tragic depression or madness in Shakespeare's mental condition when he wrote *Timon*.

While reading the essays of the critics, I have often thought they deal with the work of Shakespeare as if each play were a separate unit and was planned and written about the time it was produced. For the builder-dramatist to put them on the stocks one at a time and launch them from the ways, complete from keel to deck, is a novel idea but cannot be maintained. For all we know, some of the plays were of long and steady growth. It may very well be that one or two would be in a half-finished state when he was called upon suddenly to produce a novelty to suit the taste of the groundlings. It is quite possible that *Timon of Athens* was begun years before the date set down by the critics.

That Shakespeare suffered fits of depression and passed days of gloom may be conceded, for in that respect he was just like any of his fellows, and there was enough in his life to cause a despondent mood. For him the time was out of joint, and he realized it was useless to attempt to set it right. He had been in London long enough to know that neither Queen nor chancellors, nobility nor proletariat, Parliament nor pulpit had succeeded in undoing the wrongs of the House of Tudor.

The Golden Age was past. It was merely a memory now. The great sea dogs were scouring the oceans for plunder, and large-scale business promised big returns to those who enjoyed the monopolies and shared the wealth brought to England's shores from the New World. But I cannot agree with the notions of some of the critics who would have the poet mad when he wrote *Timon*, and weary and despondent when he wrote *The Winter's Tale*.

Perhaps, in the chorus of *Henry VIII* we may be able to

discover what was in his mind, and had been there since he was a boy. Even if this play is a joint work, shared with some other dramatist, we may be sure that the prologue was written by Shakespeare:

> I come no more to make you laugh: things now,
> That bear a weighty and a serious brow,
> Sad, high, and working, full of state and woe,
> Such noble scenes as draw the eye to flow,
> We now present. . . . .
> And if you can be merry then, I'll say
> A man may weep upon his wedding day.

Ingratitude is the theme of *King Lear* and *Timon of Athens*. In the former, Cordelia suffers because she is honest. Her sisters receive great gifts from their father because they have flattered him. These double-faced miscreants enjoy their ill-gotten gains for a time, and soon repay their father by turning him out of house and home.

In *Timon* we have a similar condition of affairs. A rich Athenian has squandered his substance upon his friends. He has given them lands, saved them from bankruptcy, presented them with horses, jewels and other valuables. He has entertained them lavishly at banquets. All this he does to satisfy his desire of making his friends happy. He asks nothing from them but good fellowship. When he has ruined himself, he turns to them for temporary aid, but finds not one willing to assist him. The consequence is that Timon, like Lear, is turned out of house and home and wanders into the wilderness to subsist on roots. In his case he has no fool to keep him company; he is alone. His steward has warned him repeatedly about the grave state of his affairs, but he has given no heed to the crumbling condition of his fortunes. This is the figure of a reckless wastrel, and typifies the state, which bribes its supporters and gives aid to its allies. Such a condition prevailed in England when Henry VII died, and it was worse after his son and Wolsey had had their day.

As with a man of prudence, so should it be with a state; neither should waste its substance. This lesson is voiced in almost cruel denunciations by several of the characters. To point the moral, we have the caustic philosopher in Apemantus. Churlish he is in thought and speech, but the goddess of wisdom was never polite. Indeed, she vied with Nemesis in being brutally candid.

It is a bitter pill our poet asks us to swallow. Those who have a sentimental feeling for the frailties of mankind may protest against his pessimistic view of affairs, but history, unfortunately, presents us with a picture of men painted in drab colors. Here and there, the one or two in a generation who hearken to the voice of Pallas Athene, are scarcely characters a dramatist can use with any success. The groundlings prefer the Iagos, the Edmunds, the Aarons—all those despicable creatures who conspire against virtue and love.

The milk of human kindness is so great a rarity, when truly proffered without thought of gain, that it is wholly without dramatic value for the stage. Indeed, in all the tragedies, virtue shines but fitfully through the murk of crime. Think of Cordelia and Ophelia, and their sisters of virtue, and try to add another without blemish.

The sentimentalist moves in a world of his own making. Usually he is a man who has known little vicissitude. He is comfortably ensconced in a home where his physical needs are satisfied each day. His position in society is such that his friends have never to be tested. Only too often they are beings who pity the poor, and keep as far from them as subscriptions to charitable institutions permit. But for the mass, life is quite different, and those who go through it without bandages on their eyes see things in their nakedness. So Apemantus, the true friend of Timon, sums it up in a verse:

> Immortal gods, I crave no pelf;
> I pray for no man but myself:
> Grant I may never prove so fond,

To trust man on his oath or bond;
Or a harlot for her weeping;
Or a dog that seems a-sleeping;
Or a keeper with my freedom;
Or my friends if I should need 'em.
Amen. So fall to 't:
Rich men sin, and I eat root.[6]

The problem of the worth of friends who have enjoyed the largesse of a rich man in time of need was no new one. There had been many cases of utter ingratitude in the lifetime of the Shakespeare family. No dramatist, at the beginning of the seventeenth century, would have had difficulty in finding in Juvenal or Seneca instances of the flimsiness of the thread that binds friends. Montaigne was at hand to supply his opinion freely of the dangers of placing too much faith in men. And surely the histories Shakespeare used for his dramas provided innumerable instances of broken faith and conspiracy against benefactors.

Apemantus was that rarity—a frank friend. But neither wise counsel nor bitter comment could prevail against Timon's belief in the goodness of man. Here is part of the speech he makes at a banquet:

.... O you gods! think I, what need we have any friends, if we should n'er have need of 'em? they were the most needless creatures living should we ne'er have use for 'em, and would most resemble sweet instruments hung up in cases, that keep their sounds to themselves. Why, I have often wished myself poorer that I might come nearer to you. We are born to do benefits; and what better or properer can we call our own than the riches of our friends? O! what a precious comfort 'tis, to have so many, like brothers, commanding one another's fortunes. ....[7]

[6] Act I, scene 2.
[7] *Ibid.*

No madman wrote this speech of a lunatic. Timon knows
not what he spends; he squanders his wealth, as if it were
drawn from a bottomless El Dorado. He is deaf to the complaints of his steward. The scenes in the second and third
acts, in which the sad plight of Timon is revealed to the
friends who have taken his gifts, are mercilessly realistic in
their vividness. What man who has known misfortune, and
through force of sheer need has stooped to test a friend, has
not found such people as Lucilius and Sempronius? The ex-
cuses they make for their inability to aid Timon are ancient
and modern. The servant of Timon, after his interview with
Sempronius, sums it up in bitter words:

> . . . . The devil knew not what he did when he made
> man politic; he crossed himself by 't: and I cannot
> think but in the end the villanies of man will set him
> clear. How fairly this lord strives to appear foul! takes
> virtuous copies to be wicked, like those that under hot
> ardent zeal would set whole realms on fire:
>
>> Of such a nature is his politic love.
>> This was my lord's best hope; now all are fled
>> Save only the gods. Now his friends are dead.[8]

Without bag or baggage, Timon leaves the city and, once
outside the walls, he delivers his curse upon it. He takes to
the woods, "where he shall find the unkindest beast more
kinder than mankind." A cave near the seashore becomes his
refuge, and in the fourth act we find him digging for roots
as provender. Suddenly the spade strikes a hoard of gold.
This discovery brings no paean of joy from him, for he
knows what the possession of it is worth:

. . . . This will make black white, foul fair,
Wrong right, base noble, old young, coward valiant.
Ha! you gods, why this? What this, you gods? Why, this
Will lug your priests and servants from your sides,
Pluck stout men's pillows from their head:

[8] Act III, scene 4.

This yellow slave
Will knit and break religions; bless the accurs'd;
Make the hoar leprosy ador'd; place thieves,
And give them title, knee, and approbation,
With senators on the bench. . . . .[9]

Other men, quite sane, have held similar ideas about the
metal, though they have not labeled its power in such trench-
ant terms.

Soon the news reaches the city that Timon has gold again.
Soldiers, whores, thieves, painters, poets seek him out in the
wilds to share some of the treasure trove. But—and here is
a discovery of transcendent worth—Flavius, his steward,
comes to him, and Timon realizes he is an honest man. He
can scarcely believe that such a creature exists.

It almost turns my dangerous nature mild.
Let me behold thy face. Surely, this man
Was born of woman.
Forgive my general and exceptless rashness,
You perpetual sober gods! I do proclaim
One honest man, mistake me not, but one;
No more, I pray, and he's a steward.[10]

Timon succeeded where Diogenes failed. Whether this is
an unfinished play or not, it seems to me that Shakespeare did
all he could with the character of Timon. What more can
be said? Who would have him brought back to Athens to
meet the friends who gathered at his table and took his gifts?
Having found an honest man, his labor is ended; but when
the cringing senators come to him, pleading with him to return, he will have none of it. He hopes that Alcibiades will
capture Athens. He tells the obsequious senators:

But yet I love my country, and am not
One that rejoices in the common wrack,
As common bruit does put it.[11]

[9] Act IV, scene 3.
[10] *Ibid.*
[11] Act V, scene 1.

He prefers death to the fate of returning to Athens as a wealthy man who will save the city. He writes his own epitaph. Alcibiades reads the inscription: "Here lies a wretched corse, of wretched soul bereft." [12]

I may be quite wrong in thinking that this play was the reverse side of a shield, and that *The Tempest* was the other. The poet poured out his wrath in the one, and then set to work to find a solution for the evils of men, which had been in his mind since he was a boy. He had bottled up his rage while he was in London, saving himself from the controversies and conspiracies of the Tudor period by constant and intensive work upon the plays and the search for the material he used. He gave himself no time for affairs other than those of the theater.

His work day must have been a long one. There is no record of persistent industry to compare with it, for it must be remembered that he was dramatist, producer, actor, and manager. How he performed all these functions and kept his health is a mystery. I have rehearsed three plays at a time but have been so exhausted after the performance of the one running at my theater that I dropped on the sofa in my room and slept without taking off my clothes. So it may be accepted by the reader that I am qualified to understand what Shakespeare's life was; and it must not be forgotten that he did not have the hundred and one aids which now shorten the labors of those who produce plays.

When he finished *Timon*, he must have held the hope that there was some way out of this chaotic state of affairs. For years he had been wading through a quagmire—the London of the Tudors. He knew that both Henry VII and his son had begun their reigns with the promise of a better state of affairs in the realm. He knew they were keen for the New Learning and gave it their support. And we may assume he

[12] *Ibid.*, scene 4.

thought their efforts at reform gave hope to those who remembered when the law and custom of the land had been sacrosanct. But the itch for war plagued both monarchs and was one cause of their undoing.

Perhaps William had heard from his father his grandfather's story of Colet denouncing war from the pulpit of St. Paul's, when he exclaimed, "An unjust peace is better than the justest war." Similar ideas are expressed in the histories.

But it was not only war; there were many grievances besides, which caused cruel strife, and the religious one was not the least of these. Hence, when he shook the dust of London from his feet, and sought the quiet of the place of his birth and boyhood, he turned his mind to the fancy of a return of happier days.

Eight

SOME PHILOSOPHICAL
CONCEPTS OF *THE TEMPEST*

THE DOMINANT MOTIF of *The Tempest* is not the taming of a savage, spawned by a witch and propagated by the devil. Such a subject might put the pen of a novelist to work, but it does not contain the material for the making of a drama. Caliban is really an accident, and stands entirely apart from the vicissitude that Prospero has endured. Even if Caliban had succeeded in raping Miranda and if she had borne an offspring, semi-savage, that alone would scarcely have served Shakespeare as a subject for a play.

Caliban came into the life of the magician when he reached the island, after being cast adrift by his brother. The savage was in no way concerned with the conspiracy in Milan of a usurper and Prospero's political enemy, the King of Naples. To regard this secondary feature of the play from this standpoint does not detract in any way from the interest of what might be done to civilize a sub-human creature.

Let us consider the interesting problem of the proprietorship of the island. Robert Speaight, in *Nature in Shakespearian Tragedy*, touches the rim of this notion, when he says:

> . . . . We should remember that before the providential seas washed up Prospero on the shores of the island, Caliban was the master of it; and Caliban would always regard Prospero as a usurper. . . . .

And so, during the twelve years which have elapsed

since the sea first took a decisive hand in the business, Prospero and Miranda have arrived at the power of something very like perfection. . . . . Prospero has gained possession of the isle, and this is very literally a victory of mind over matter. The Elizabethans—and Shakespeare with them—had scant regard for aboriginal rights. Prospero derives his title from the intrinsic superiority of civilized man over savages, and Caliban is very properly reduced to his natural status of slavery. . . . .[1]

Speaight overlooks the question of rights in this respect: Would Caliban have conceded the same right of life to Prospero, as he arrogated to himself, if he had been the stronger? In all cases of imperialism recorded in English history down to the nineteenth century, the stranger has succeeded in depriving the native of his right to use the land for his material well-being. It was well put by the head of a tribe in South Africa: "Before you came, you had the Bible and we had the land; after you had been here a short time, you had the land and we had the Bible."

I think this problem of proprietorship on the island is one with which Shakespeare was familiar in Warwickshire. The enclosures round about Welcombe and other districts were matters of deep concern to the people. In *The Tempest* the question of proprietorship may be described as the perpetual one of: *Who is to rule?* It is unthinkable that a civilized man would become the slave of a savage. But, in this case, Prospero had not the slightest intention of invading the island and taking possession of it.

In reading the above quotation from Speaight's book, I wondered how an informed man could make such a statement as "Caliban is very properly reduced to his natural status of slavery." Surely this controverts every fundamental idea of primitive economic conditions held by Sir Henry Maine and many other learned investigators. When and

[1] Pp. 157-8.

where was there a *natural* status of slavery? It was Prospero who made a slave of Caliban. Before the magician came to the island, the savage was free—just as free as the savages of dark Africa before the Christians of European countries appropriated their natural resources and enslaved them.

Speaight contradicts himself, for if he grants that natives have aboriginal rights, he cannot maintain his statement about a "natural status of slavery."

The significance of Caliban is of such economic and sociological importance that I begin to wonder if Shakespeare, by some intuition, placed him at the very center of the plot. It is no exaggeration to say that he makes the play. This fact has not always been appreciated by many of the critics. One wonders, also, whether the poet was quite conscious of Caliban's peculiar economic function as the only chore man of Prospero, in contrast to the educated conspirators.

The student grounded in the fundamentals of the production of wealth will recognize in this creature the trace of an economic philosophy based upon the primary factors of wealth—land and labor. (The third factor—capital, or tools of the most primitive order—is not considered because there is no direct reference to such an aid in the play.) Neither Prospero nor Miranda reveals, in speech or action, that one or the other assists in finding food. Caliban seems to be the sole producer, and one wonders what his master and his daughter would have done to sustain life if there had been no Caliban to fend for them.

In our attempt to examine the utility of Caliban, we should recognize that he is gifted with all the senses. He may be half fish, bred by the devil and a witch, but he can speak, taste, see, feel and smell, and is equipped with arms and hands. Moreover, he is educable, for both Miranda and her father tell us quite clearly how they have tried to instruct him. So his origin as a land animal is not altered in any way, for he cannot exist without food, fuel, clothing and shelter.

In this, he differs from Ariel, who was imprisoned in the pine tree by Sycorax, and yet lived for twelve years. But then Ariel is not human, in any way. He must subsist on manna dropped from heaven, which we cannot believe is shared by Prospero and his daughter.

What was the provender that kept these people alive? We learn from Caliban that he knew all the qualities of the island. He knew fertile land from that which was arid. In the scene with the drunken Stephano and Trinculo, he tells us of berries, fish, the best fresh springs, crabs, pig-nuts, eggs of birds, marmosets, filberts, and mussels. In the play, these last (which cling to rocks) are called scamels, and the term has given many of the critics cause for unnecessary speculation as to what a scamel is. This is a catalogue of fish and of natural fruits, and we must infer that these have supplied the larder for the three earthly beings. Caliban, then, is the most useful member of that small community.

It is not necessary to waste a sentimental moment upon the lot of this character. In all the history of native lands grabbed by pagan or Christian imperialists, the record is almost bare of anyone who wasted a tear upon the lot of the savages who had to be civilized. During the nineteenth century it was taken as a matter of course, and many were the prayers offered up for the salvation of their dark souls. Now the white man's burden is crushing him, and the displacement of individuals of another color and their migration to the countries of white people is a sore problem in many lands.

In considering this matter of who owns the island, we should not overlook the peculiar plight of Prospero and his infant child. She is to be protected at all costs. Whether the magician had the power to place her in a charmed circle, which could not be penetrated by a savage, we are not informed. The natural instinct of Caliban to crave sexual satisfaction would always be in the thought of Prospero, and this matter must be kept in mind when the problem of proprietorship is raised. It is a feeling entirely different in nature from the usurpation of his brother, Antonio, in Milan. The fate of his child is ever present, and her happiness, which is her virtue, beats with every throb of her father's heart.

To what extent Shakespeare was indebted to Montaigne for ideas dramatized in *The Tempest* has always been a matter that has stirred up widely different opinions among the scholars. Some of them think it was the narratives of the sea rovers from which he took his material. This question is still being debated and no definite conclusion has been reached. One way of deciding whether to accept or reject the suggestion is to read the play and then take up Montaigne's *Essays* and study his chapter, "Of the Caniballes." [2] Here may be found some of the material which prompted the creation of Caliban and the nature of the island on which Prospero was cast adrift.

Montaigne's *Essays* were very popular in England, for they were translated into the language of its people by John Florio. One copy in the British Museum has a signature on the fly-leaf "Willm. Shakspere," which some authorities do not accept as genuine. Still, the skeptics admit that there are passages in *The Tempest* which indicate that Shakespeare was acquainted with Montaigne's work. Some of the scholars have conceded it was quite probable that he knew John Florio through their common patron, Southampton. The date of Florio's translation is 1603; modern critics place *The Tempest* in 1611. Shakespeare would have had time enough to read the work.

One passage from Montaigne, on Cannibals, must have made our poet think of those who enjoyed the shows at

[2] N.Y.: Carlton House, n.d., first series, chap. xxx. It is interesting to note that Shakespeare, as early as 1604, in *Othello*, speaks of Cannibals:

> And of the Cannibals that each other eat,
> The Anthropophagi, and men whose heads
> Do grow beneath their shoulders.
>
> (Act I, scene 3)

Tyburn. It refers to the atrocities perpetrated by the Portuguese:

> . . . . I am not sorie we note the barbarous horror of such an action, but grieved, that prying so narrowly into their faults we are so blinded in ours. I thinke there is more barbarisme in eating men alive, then to feed upon them, being dead; to mangle by tortures and torments a body full of lively sense, to roast him in peeces, to make dogges and swine to gnaw and teare him in mammockes (as wee have not only read but seene very lately, yea and our own memorie, not amongst ancient enemies, but our neighbours and fellow-citizens; and which is worse, under pretence of pietie and religion) than to roast and eat him after he is dead. . . . .[3]

According to Montaigne, barbarism was not a pastime practiced only by the uncivilized, nor did he think it was an ancient one limited to pagans. It is an amusing exercise to read Montaigne's essay after studying *The Tempest*.

In More's *Utopia*, Shakespeare would also find very different stories of lands beyond the Atlantic from those given by the sea rovers and their scribes. The account of the voyages of Raphael Hythloday, in the first book of *Utopia* would rivet his attention and kindle in his mind thoughts of a Golden Age.

> [Hythloday] joyned himself in company with Amerike Vespuce, and in the iii. last voyages of those iiii. that be nowe in printe and abrode in every mannes handes, he continued styll in his company, savyng that in the last voyage he came not home agayne with him. . . . .[4]

The adventures of some of Vespucci's crew, after their captain departed, are of peculiar interest to the student of *The Tempest*. Hythloday says they began to win the love and favor of the people, and within a short time dwelt among

[3] *Ibid.*, pp. 166-7.
[4] P. 4.

them without harm, for the natives of that country lived together in a civil policy and good order. And here we learn
something of savages—the Calibans of uncivilized lands:

> . . . . Nothyng is more easye to bee founde, then
> bee barkynge Scyllaes, ravenyng Celenes, and Lestri-
> gones devourers of people, and suche lyke great, and
> incredible monsters. But to fynde Citisens ruled by
> good and holsome lawes, that is an exceeding rare, and
> harde thyng. . . . .[5]

There is much in *The Tempest* that reflects the ideas of
Montaigne and Sir Thomas More.

Setting aside the secondary plot of *The Tempest*, let us
now consider the dominant one, that is, bringing Prospero's
enemies to heel. For twelve years he has waited for the
chance to take revenge upon his brother and the King of
Naples for casting him and his child adrift. At last he learns
of their visit to Tunis for the marriage of the King's daughter. How he became possessed of this information is not
clear, but he tells Miranda:

> By accident most strange, bountiful Fortune,
> . . . . hath mine enemies
> Brought to this shore; and by my prescience
> I find my zenith doth depend upon
> A most auspicious star, whose influence
> If now I court not, but omit, my fortunes
> Will ever after droop. . . . .[6]

By some form of telepathy he has learned of the return
voyage, and, magically, has intercepted the King's ship and
created, with the aid of Ariel, a raging storm which has
driven the vessel ashore.

Now that he has cast a spell upon them, and Ariel is carry-

[5] *Ibid.*, p. 8.
[6] Act I, scene 2.

ing out his plan of making them realize their bitter plight, the chief problem of the play looms up like a flash. How will he be avenged? What punishment will be meted out to them? This is perhaps the gravest question that arises in any of the plays in which we have had samples of nearly every kind of penalty inflicted upon a culprit, innocent or guilty. Shakespeare must have known his Bible, and in the Pentateuch he could read of many atrocious sentences passed upon enemies:

> For a fire is kindled in mine anger. . . . .
> They shall be burnt with hunger, and devoured with burning heat, and with bitter destruction: I will also send the teeth of beasts upon them, with the poison of serpents of the dust.
> I will make mine arrows drunk with blood, and my sword shall devour flesh; and that with the blood of the slain and of the captives, from the beginning of revenges upon the enemy.[7]

The atrocities of vengeance have a long history. Shakespeare might have asked himself what all the punishments of the Tudors had done to bring about a reign of justice. Certainly enough blood was spilled during the Wars of the Roses and the reigns of the usurping bastard's family to show whether vindictive revenge put fear into the hearts of evildoers. Thus, early in the play the question is: What power will he exert, when he takes his revenge upon his brother, Antonio, and his enemy, the Duke of Milan?

We do not know he has a weapon until the last act. There is no torture machine on the island. They are many—a king's retinue, the master and crew of the ship. Prospero is alone, for Caliban would be of little use against the swords of his master's enemies. The second scene of Act One is a masterpiece of ingenuity in creating perplexity and curiosity in the minds of the audience.

---

[7] Deut. 32:22, 24, 42.

This theme of vengeance appears strongly in *Titus Andronicus*. There, foul play is shown in all its horror. The deeds of Aaron and Tamora are as awful as the imagination can conceive, and Titus, who has borne the brunt of detestable crime, cries aloud for power to avenge his wrongs.

However, in the fourth act there is a note that couples revenge with justice. Here it is:

Pub.   . . . . Pluto sends you word,
If you will have Revenge from hell, you shall:
Marry, for Justice, she is so employ'd,
He thinks, with Jove in heaven, or somewhere else,
So that perforce you must needs stay a time.
Tit.   He doth me wrong to feed me with delays.
I'll dive into the burning lake below,
And pull her out of Acheron by the heels.
Marcus, we are but shrubs, no cedars we;
No big-bon'd men fram'd of the Cyclops' size;
But metal, Marcus, steel to the very back,
Yet wrung with wrongs more than our backs can bear:
And sith there's no justice in earth nor hell,
We will solicit heaven and move the gods
To send down Justice for to wreak our wrongs.[8]

Soliciting heaven to send down justice, to assist Titus to carry out his plan of vengeance, is a cry of desperation that chills the blood. Does it mean there is no earthly power to curb wrong and establish right, and that all that can be done to bring about an effective result is to rely upon a supernatural agent? As Christians, we have been bred up to the notion that heavenly justice will have no mercy upon unrepentant sinners.

If Shakespeare did read his Bible, he would find the first chapter of Romans a comprehensive text for the treatment of evildoers. Paul, here, gives us an account of the punishments they should expect in good measure:

[8] Scene 4.

For the wrath of God is revealed from heaven against all ungodliness and unrighteousness of men, who hold the truth in unrighteousness;

And even as they did not like to retain God in their knowledge, God gave them over to a reprobate mind, to do those things which are not convenient;

Being filled with all unrighteousness, fornication, wickedness, covetousness, maliciousness; full of envy, murder, debate, deceit, malignity; whisperers,

Backbiters, haters of God, despiteful, proud, boasters, inventors of evil things, disobedient to parents.[9]

The pilgrim from Tarsus believed in vengeance by the wholesale. Many of his victims were people who did not agree with his mission or his methods of prosecuting it. Still, it must be admitted his notions of vengeance were well grounded in ancient precedents. Think of what Homer revealed in the *Iliad* about the row over the abduction of a woman. In this history of Troy, he lets us know that the gods themselves have ways of meting out vengeance even upon their own kin.

So when the rage of Xanthos was overcome, both ceased, for Hera stayed them, though in wrath. But among the other gods fell grievous bitter strife, and their hearts were carried diverse in their breasts. And they clashed together with a great noise, and the wide earth groaned, and the clarion of great Heaven rang around. Zeus heard as he sate upon Olympus, and his heart within him laughed pleasantly when he beheld that strife of gods. Then no longer stood they asunder, for Ares piercer of shields began the battle and first made for Athene with his bronze spear, and spake a taunting word: "Wherefore, O dogfly, dost thou match gods with gods in strife, with stormy daring, as thy great spirit moveth thee? Rememberest thou not how thou movedst Diomedes Tydeus' son to wound me, and thyself didst take a visible spear and thrust it

[9] Rom. 1:18, 28, 29, 30.

straight at me and pierce through my fair skin? Therefore deem I now that thou shalt pay me for all that thou hast done."

Thus saying he smote on the dread tasselled aegis that not even the lightning of Zeus can overcome— thereon smote bloodstained Ares with his long spear. But she, giving back, grasped with stout hand a stone that lay upon the plain, black, rugged, huge, which men of old time set to be the landmark of a field; this hurled she, and smote impetuous Ares on the neck, and unstrung his limbs. Seven roods he covered in his fall, and soiled his hair with dust, and his armour rang upon him. And Pallas Athene laughed, and spake to him winged words exultingly: "Fool, not even yet hast thou learnt how far better than thou I claim to be, that thus thou matchest thy might with mine.[10]

It is rather shocking for a Christian to learn that this pagan dispenser of justice laughed at what was taking place. Of course, he was exempt from retaliatory vengeance, having given himself a license to sin when and how he liked. Yet, there is this disturbing thought: if justice is not to be found even in the pagan heaven (the one Titus called on), is it reasonable to hope for it to descend from a Christian one? Surely we understand that, if you violate a law of nature, you will pay the penalty.

Oddly enough, a performance of *Titus Andronicus* was recently given at the Shakespeare Memorial Theatre at Stratford upon Avon, and scholars from a dozen different countries assembled there to see the play. Professor Eugene Waith of Yale University took for his subject the metamorphosis of violence, and according to the report in *The Times* (London), said:

> The theme of *Titus Andronicus* was the opposition
> of moral and political disorder to the unifying force

[10] English Prose Version by Andrew Lang, Walter Leaf and Ernest Myers (N.Y.: Modern Library, n.d.), Book XXI, pp. 393-4.

of friendship and wise government, a theme in which Shakespeare was interested all his life.

I congratulate the professor, for it is the first time I ever remember seeing the theme stated so simply and plainly by a Shakespearian critic.

Modern critics place *Titus Andronicus* in the year 1594. Furnivall dated it five years earlier, immediately after *Love's Labour's Lost*. This indicates that Shakespeare, early in his career as a dramatist, had a desire to show the futility of punishing crime by violent crime. All the tragedies are permeated with this idea. Think of the last scene of *Coriolanus*, when the conspirators cry: "Kill, kill, kill, kill, kill him!" Then they turn upon Coriolanus and slay him. His foe, Aufidius, stands upon the body, and one of the lords says: "Thou hast done a deed whereat valour will weep." Another one says: "Let him be regarded as the most noble corse that ever herald did follow to his urn."

Now comes an amazing revulsion in the mind of Aufidius:

> My rage is gone,
> And I am struck with sorrow. Take him up:
> Help, three o' the chiefest soldiers; I'll be one.[11]

This play appeared fourteen years after *Titus*.

I cannot believe that Shakespeare, with Montaigne upon his knee, could have overlooked Chapter XXXI in the *Essays:* "That a Man Ought Soberly to Meddle with Judging of Divine Lawes." We learn there of the death of Arrius and Pope Leo. Heliogabalus was also slain in a privy. The wise old skeptic found it no easy matter to reduce divine things unto our balance. He sums up the matter as Shakespeare did in his plays:

> . . . . Gods intent being to teach us, that the good
> have some thing else to hope for, and the wicked some-

[11] Act V, scene 5.

what else to feare, than the good or bad fortune of this world: He manageth and applieth them according to his secret disposition: and depriveth us of the meanes, thereby foolishly to make our profit. And those, that according to humane reason will thereby prevaile, doe but mocke themselves. . . . .[12]

Montaigne knew his Bible, and I daresay, when he wrote the chapter referred to above, he might have been thinking of Deuteronomy:

To me belongeth vengeance, and recompence; their foot shall slide in due time: for the day of their calamity is at hand, and the things that shall come upon them make haste.[13]

This question of vengeance and its consequences should be gone into more thoroughly. Shakespeare shows that he had fathomed all its tests before he wrote *The Tempest*. In *Hamlet* he said all there was to be said about it and what it leads to. For, is not the hesitant Prince of Denmark a symbol of the philosophy of our poet?

[12] Pp. 172-3.
[13] 32:35.

Nine

THE THEME
OF FOUL PLAY

To WANDER THROUGH the bewildering maze created by Shakespearian critics since the days of Coleridge is an arduous trek for anyone who wishes to reach a point of observation from which he may view an unlittered scene, clear of entangling undergrowth. If one desires to see the mountains in full view, the mighty peaks of the greatest dramatic poet, it would be well to read the plays without comment or footnotes. This is what the actors had to do when the plays were performed under the direction of Shakespeare himself, and this is what all actors have had to do since that day. Words no longer in use, broken passages, involved sentences are matters dealt with at rehearsal, and somehow the men engaged in the production find an acceptable way out of their difficulties.

I have never known any book of reference to be used at rehearsal except the glossary, which can be had in almost any edition of the plays. These remarks are prompted by my own experience of comparing at least ten or twelve different opinions about the play and its parts. For anyone interested in the diversity of ideas about it—its construction, its intention and aim, the spelling, the punctuation, the metrical blunders, and its sources, the Arden Shakespeare will well suffice for that purpose.

If Shakespeare had been burdened with one-tenth of the

notions held by the critics, the play would never have been written. How does a dramatist go to work? For the theater of today, as I know it, the author devises a plot, and puts characters in it to work it out. Often enough, plays are written for a particular actor or actress. Those of us over sixty remember the period of tailor-made plays, the days when Arthur Pinero and Henry Arthur Jones wrote their greatest successes for actor-managers.

But no play of Shakespeare came about in this way. His plots arise out of the clash of characters. Take the tragedies: Othello against Iago, Lear against his kin, Hamlet against the King; and Macbeth against Banquo, with the witches to devise the scheme. In each case, the plot is carried by the characters to the very end.

The eminence of our poet is not diminished when we say that the dominant idea which possessed him when he wrote the tragedies was action and, as an actor, he knew his audience would demand it. The very lines he wrote and the language he used bespeak action. I daresay he began on the scenes of the first act with never a thought of what would happen in the last one. Foul play was enough to carry the drama on to the bitter end, and foul play is the key term to much of his work. The use of the word *foul* in Shakespeare is impressive. The epithet stands out in scene after scene. It appears in all the tragedies, in *Hamlet*, in *Macbeth*, in *Othello*, and in *King Lear*. And oddly enough, it is the theme of *The Tempest*.

The use of this word in the tragedies comes from the mind of one who has suffered. When Lear realizes, in the third act, the woe his vanity has brought upon his head, he cries:

> . . . . Here I stand, your slave,
> A poor, infirm, weak, and despis'd old man.
> But yet I call you servile ministers,
> That have with two pernicious daughters join'd

> Your high-engender'd battles 'gainst a head
> So old and white as this. O! O! 'tis foul.[1]

In *Othello*, Brabantio denounces Othello: "O thou foul thief! Where hast thou stow'd my daughter?" [2]

Then, before the Senate, Othello exclaims:

> If you do find me foul in her report,
> The trust, the office I do hold of you,
> Not only take away, but let your sentence
> Even fall upon my life.[3]

After the death of Desdemona, Othello cries, "O! she was foul." [4]

In *Macbeth* we find the term in the earliest scene, when the witches cry, "Fair is foul and foul is fair." The first line Macbeth speaks is: "So foul and fair a day I have not seen." [5]

In the opening act of *Hamlet* the word comes frequently: "I doubt some foul play"; then it is repeated in the same speech: "Foul deeds will rise." The Ghost uses it several times.

The theme of foul play and its consequences runs through all the tragedies. The epithet must have been deeply embedded in the mind of Shakespeare, for in the histories he saw it practiced by high and low, and as many of the characters prophesied, it meant nothing but ill for England. Long before he wrote the tragedies, Shakespeare's soul must have revolted at the misdeeds of royal kin, of nobles of power, and their servitors. Small wonder that, toward the end, he desired to rid his mind of memories that had darkened so much of his life.

But London was scarcely the place in which he would find

[1] Act III, scene 2.
[2] Act I, scene 2.
[3] Act I, scene 3.
[4] Act V, scene 2.
[5] Act I, scene 3.

the atmosphere to cleanse his thought. He had been a slave to Melpomene and Thalia for many years, and at their bidding had given his world the finest jewels of his genius. He had made occasional trips to Stratford during the busy years, and we note in many of the plays that he was familiar with the vagabonds and thieves of the highways.

Autolycus in *The Winter's Tale* speaks of hangings. Richard Hakluyt lived when Shakespeare was at work, and he has recorded: "For small robberies [able men] are daily hanged . . . . even twenty at a clap out of some one gaol." We can imagine what Shakespeare thought about the sight of gibbets along roads as he journeyed back and forth from London.

In *Henry VIII* we learn of the troubles of the clothiers, many of whom were "constrained out of service." Sir John Clapham, in his *Concise Economic History of Britain*, points out how Wolsey's changes of international fiscal policy "have put off the spinsters, carders, fullers, weavers" and that great multitudes of these clothiers were idle. An old ballad reminds us that "men sigh and sob" for work.[6]

Then there was all the trouble about enclosures, and although our polite historians treat the matter lightly, George M. Trevelyan in *English Social History* says, "These forms of enclosure . . . . especially the enclosure of commons, were deeply resented, and provoked riot and rebellion." [7]

There was enough, and more, of travail and discontent in London and in the country to sicken the heart of a man who had heard of the prosperous days of the English laborer, which came after the Black Death.

No man could have characterized so sharply the folk of Eastcheap, of country inns, of London's taverns, unless there was a sympathetic bond between him and them. No person wedded to the aristocracy and the life at court could have

[6] Cambridge University Press, 1949, p. 250.
[7] London and N.Y.: Longmans, Green & Co., 1942, p. 116.

drawn portraits so unmistakably real as Mistress Quickly, Bardolph, Pistol, and the many others of their kidney that appear in the histories. George Bernard Shaw and those who think with him that Shakespeare was a servile creature of the upper crust of society have not read very closely the poet's works.

The district round about Stratford suffered from forcible enclosures. It had a long history. The dissolution of the abbeys was quite another affair. The vast areas that Burghley, the Russells, the Fitzwilliams, and other sycophants of Henry VIII's court took possession of must have exceeded the rosiest dreams of land avarice. Many of the abbots themselves were guilty of enclosure, and we have records of their being greedy landlords. But, though agriculture was supposed to benefit by the change, the passing of the land from the monastics to the laymen gave the people no better landlords and turned loose upon the highway the vagabonds and thieves that More describes in *Utopia*.

It is nonsense to imagine that agriculture was benefited by the change. The documents of the time show clearly that many were the complaints about turning arable land to pasture for sheep. The production of meat and dairy products from cattle suffered, and it was not until long years after that the growing of crops and the raising of animals marked a change in the general purposes of agriculture.

Progress, as it was considered after the Renaissance, when the mercantile system popped up its ugly head, was a Janus-faced creature, and Shakespeare, looking back over the awful record of what the change had meant, set down in *The Tempest* quite a different system. To my mind, this play demonstrates clearly that Shakespeare had read his Bible and remembered the promise of Isaiah:

> They shall not build, and another inhabit; they shall
> not plant, and another eat: for as the days of a tree are

the days of my people, and mine elect shall long enjoy
the work of their hands.[8]

They shall "enjoy the work of their hands," not under a
system of landlordism, in which the one who neither toils
nor spins takes the first share. It is all very well and good
for those who plead that Shakespeare desired order within
the realm to attribute to him a full-hearted desire for it. But
a country lad, who knew what he did of the fields and the
harvests of producers, was as keen for an economic order for
the peasantry as he was for that of the court. He never for-
got the farmer, for his forebears had tilled the land and loved
it. He presents the peasant with his feet on the soil; the
tongue he speaks is that of the shire; his humor is that of the
farm; and the homeliness of his thought indicates that only
the poor can be kind to the poor. We have that in play after
play. It is richly described in *As You Like It*, in *The Winter's Tale*, and other of the pastoral comedies, to say nothing of some of the classical plays.

Stratford! Think of the longing he must have had for
home, to take his ease at his own fireside and meditate upon
what might have been. To have his own house and be master
of the hours must have been the fulfillment of a dream he
had held since he was a lad.

When I was a boy, the old folks would say, "You can
never outlive the smell of the soil," and perhaps the odor of
it after rain. The scent of new-mown grass must have been
in his nostrils even when he presented a play at court. All
this is redolent in his work. A lad who had roamed the
ditches and knew the blooms that spring brought forth there
was the man who wrote the great poems of foul play, of ingratitude, of conspiracies to gain power, of kin against kin,
of unnatural deed. And no other could have done it.

If there were visits to Stratford during the periods when

[8] 65:22.

the theaters were closed and during the years when the plague visited London, it is reasonable to think that he would have time to give to a play. With no rehearsals to attend, he would have a full day for writing. He must have longed for such uninterrupted days—perhaps weeks—in the quiet of his own house. He was an owner of land and property when his father died in 1601. The next year he wrote three plays.

In the historical order set out in the Oxford Shakespeare, they were *All's Well That Ends Well*, *Troilus and Cressida*, and *Hamlet*. Again I must remind the reader that the dates given to the plays by the modern critics refer only to their appearance. So far, no one has given an estimate of the time taken for writing each one. We do not know how long he carried the idea of *Hamlet* in his mind before he wrote the first scene. Such plays as the ones we are studying germinate slowly, like some of the symphonies and operas of which we have record.

It is my opinion that the idea of Prospero was born many years before the date of his appearance on the stage. In my analysis I hope to show some evidence of this in the play.

No one can tell the amount of work that was done at Stratford, but the need of uninterrupted hours tempts me to believe that during the last ten years of his life, Shakespeare visited Stratford each year, perhaps more than once, and accomplished what would have been impossible during the seasons at the Globe or any other theater in London.

It is strange we know so little of one so great. His life in London, apart from the business of the theater, must have been devoted to his work. He could have had no leisure for conviviality. Think of how few his cronies were. We know none save for those who were writers for the stage, such as Jonson, Greene, and others; but it may be supposed he knew Southampton and perhaps some of his friends.

Then, as now, lovers of the theater sought out dramatists

and actors, but the acquaintanceship probably did not extend beyond the stage door or the green room, if such a place was used. Actors in a stock company are busy most of the day: rehearsals in the morning; studying a part in the afternoon; and then at night the performance. Ten hours of waking time taken up with work give little chance for social affairs. As the off-season drew nigh, we may imagine how he longed for Stratford, for Susanna and Judeth were there, and his father, until 1601. There were grandchildren, besides, and other connections of the family. From the wills and other scanty documents we gather that Shakespeare was a man who thought of his own folk and took pride in their welfare.

I have often sat in the garden of the house in which it is said Shakespeare was born, and wondered if the paths were those he trod, and the turf, spotted with "daisies pied," that which kissed his feet. He lived at New Place, but I can imagine the garden of the old house would attract him.

It seemed to me when I was there, over fifty years ago (and many times since), that the spirits of the tragedies and *The Tempest* still lingered in the shadows of the place. Perhaps he sat there building the structures, scene by scene, which were later set down in the calm of the evenings, and made ready for rehearsal after his return to London. Where else could his own library have been but at Stratford? The plays themselves supply sufficient evidence of the scope of his reading.

In *Henry VI, Part I* he mentions Froissart, and in *The Tempest*, the references to Dido and Aeneas reveal his knowledge of Virgil's *Aeneid*. There is much in the play that shows he was indebted to Ovid, for Gonzalo's description of the Golden Age is derived from the first book of the *Metamorphoses*. Montaigne's *Essays*, too, he must have turned to on many occasions.

The learning revealed in the plays is not of the kind that

would be gathered by a mere boy from the works in Latin studied at school. One critic mentions Aesop's fables, Caesar, Cicero, Virgil, Horace, Plautus, Terence, and Seneca—a very large order for a mature scholar. This wide literary background substantiates my belief that, during the "lost years" when he was perhaps a chorister in a nobleman's company of players, he had the advantage of using the library of the manor.

The four plays—*Love's Labour's Lost, The Comedy of Errors, Two Gentlemen of Verona,* and *Henry VI*—all made their appearance, according to the historical order determined by modern critics, within two years. Surely this means that some of them were written before Shakespeare reached London.

Think of the labor of writing these plays. There were no typewriters, no stenographers at that time, and I cannot imagine an amanuensis of that period who would be of any assistance to Shakespeare. Concerning the sheer labor of making a play, I know from experience that one can be done in a week, but only by dictating it to an accomplished typist.

How long he was at work upon *The Tempest* no one has ventured to estimate. This is somewhat strange, because the work is one that has attracted every Shakespearian scholar since Hazlitt wrote: "*The Tempest* is one of the most original and perfect of Shakespeare's productions, and he has shown in it all the variety of his powers. It is full of grace and grandeur."

In *The New Temple Shakespeare,* edited by M. R. Ridley, we learn:

> There is no doubt that the play, presumably in the shape in which we have it, was one of the "fourteen severall playes" presented at court by John Heminge in the winter of 1612-13 as part of the celebrations for the betrothal and wedding of King James's daughter, the Princess Elizabeth, to the Prince Palatine Elector.

There is also little doubt that it was presented at Court in some shape in November 1611. . . . .[9]

It seems to me that the original play did not contain the masque, but that it was introduced to celebrate the royal marriage. That there was a reason in the play itself for such a masque I shall show later, but I doubt very much that Shakespeare thought of it until the opportunity arose for presenting it at the time of the betrothal. It seems an after-thought—"lugged in," to use the old expression of actors—although it carries out an idea that is forcibly expressed in an early scene.

I have often wondered if Shakespeare's reading of Seneca's *Medea* suggested some material for *The Tempest*. In the play by the Roman poet, we have magical power, storm-tossed ships, revenge, and other suggestive events that might have inspired the sensitive mind of the poet. With the aid of his inventive powers, he could transpose these incidents into a full symphony, in which the fourth movement becomes a benediction.

In Frank Kermode's introduction to the Arden edition of *The Tempest*, we find a brief restatement of the criticism of the experts since the days of Coleridge. None of this, how-ever, is of the slightest use to the actor, for no matter how learned the stage director might be, there is little he could impart at rehearsal to those who have to play the roles. None of it would help them. Indeed, much of it might seriously handicap them, if he made an attempt to use it. There is nothing to give him the slightest indication of how a line should be spoken, how a trait may be added to his notion of the character, or what gestures Prospero would make when he wears the magician's cloak.

Most of the criticism of the experts of our day has been devoted to problems that are beyond the consideration of the

[9] London: J. M. Dent & Sons; N.Y.; E. P. Dutton & Co., 1943, Preface, p. viii.

actor. Some say it is an allegory; others say the intention is to present Art and Nature, either in conflict or in unison. This I shall consider at length in another chapter.

The strangest notion suggested is that it expresses Christian dogma; that virtue is triumphant and forgiveness is the solution which will defeat crime. Why it should be necessary to find anything of a symbolical significance in the work, I cannot understand, for the play clearly explains itself, and I cannot imagine a groundling at the Globe, or a man in the gallery of a modern theater, asking for more information about the play when the curtain falls. He has heard the lines and he has seen the action, and its success and constant repetition give me the idea he has been satisfied with the entertainment.

The critics who regard it as a biographical drama have reason on their side, but before accepting this conclusion, we must first make a thorough survey of the thought and work of the poet, which I intend to do. The biographical idea is not in the play itself. No one reading it or seeing it acted would think, for a moment, that Shakespeare was presenting himself. Still, there is a personal philosophy in it, which is broadly based upon the thought and work of his life. It is the distillation of problems that harassed him from the days of his youth.

One more concept remains to be mentioned—the very old theme used by dramatists—the test of virtue. Kermode, in his introduction, tells us:

> There is a hint to the answer in the treatment in the play of the word "virtue," which is, as I have suggested, closely related to the nature of the noble. The noble are virtuous, as was Miranda's mother—her virtue expresses itself as chastity; this is always so in noble women. Miranda has "the very virtue of compassion," the noble essence of it. Ferdinand has admired several women for "several virtues," which he paraphrases as "noble graces." He admires Miranda because she has

all these qualities without their defects, being purely noble, the perfection of her own nature. Prospero, with true princely magnanimity, decides that the act of revenge, when at his mercy lie all his enemies, must remain undone, since "virtue" is nobler than vengeance.[10]

It is well we should understand this matter clearly because no dramatist ever put virtue to such a test as Shakespeare did. In the comedies and romances it is treated with the respect it deserves, according to the situation in the play; and "all's well that ends well," after it has served its purpose, that is, to bring the curtain down on the tag "they lived happily ever after." But virtue in the tragedies earns no reward.

Desdemona, Ophelia and Cordelia—all noble—are examples of the terrors of the test. In *Macbeth* a man suffers who

> Hath borne his faculties so meek, hath been
> So clear in his great office, that his virtues
> Will plead like angels trumpet-tongued against
> The deep damnation of his taking off. . . . .[11]

Shakespeare was the last man in the Tudor period to indulge in fanciful notions about virtue reaping reward in the real drama of life. He knew how men and women, comparatively virtuous, were executed together with those who had no virtue in them. The block, the instruments of torture, the hurdle, the gallows at Tyburn, the fires of Smithfield and Oxford were revelations that sickened his soul.

[10] *Loc. cit.*, p. liii.
[11] Act I, scene 7.

Ten

ART AND NATURE

THE WRITING OF an interpretation of one of Shakespeare's plays is a most attractive exercise for the scholar-critic. To follow the process of its development, to learn what prompted him to devise the scheme, and to divine the intention and aim of it are fascinating tasks. The student cannot read such essays and lectures as those of Bradley, Dowden, Chambers, and many other writers and escape the impression that analysis is a never-ending job.

Yet, it is possible to read their books closely and decide that there is something more to be said, even by the most intensive expert. It is in *The Tempest* I find (entirely apart from the aspect of producing the play, and its effect on an audience) another important matter to be considered. Some of the critics mentioned above have touched lightly upon it, but none, to my way of thinking, has made a thorough examination of the problem. I refer to what may be called "intention." What did the author mean to convey to us?

Before examining this, I should like to make it clear to the reader that I cannot imagine for a moment that Shakespeare troubled himself about the subtleties so profoundly discussed by the scholars. Philosophic ideas are not material for the dramatist, and I doubt whether the most skillful playwright could make a success of one whose motive was an esthetic problem. However, it might be profitable to look into the question of intention, of the functions of the characters, and what they represent in the realms of art. This quest, of course, includes the relationship of six of the principal characters. But it is my purpose to treat here only two —Prospero and Ariel—and to attempt to reach a clear understanding of these two magical characters.

Frank Kermode, in his introduction to the Arden edition of *The Tempest*, tells us:

> . . . . There is no need to labour the connexion between this romantic convention and the fitful divinization of beauty in the actual world. It corresponds to the extension of Prospero's princely powers into the realm of magic.
>
> The romantic story is, then, the mode in which Shakespeare made his last poetic investigation into the supernatural elements in the human soul and in human society. His thinking is Platonic, though never schematic; and he had deliberately chosen the pastoral tragicomedy as the genre in which this inquiry is best pursued. The pastoral romance gave him the opportunity for a very complex comparison between the worlds of Art and Nature; and the tragicomic form enabled him to concentrate the whole story of apparent disaster, penitence, and forgiveness into one happy misfortune, controlled by a divine Art.[1]

This statement raises the eternal problem of the relationship of Art to Nature. Indeed, it goes more deeply than that, for it brings to the fore the problem of explaining the mystery of the creative faculties of the human mind. And it is here we are confronted with the magical association of Prospero and Ariel.

The former servant of Sycorax deserves more consideration in this respect than he gets from the scholars. Surely a student of the play must gather from it that Ariel is the essential, active agent of the desires of his master. It would not be surprising if the student should ask: Would Prospero

[1] Pp. lviii-lix.

have been able to accomplish such a feat as the wreck of the ship, if there had been no Ariel? Frank Kermode says:

> The main opposition is between the worlds of Prospero's Art, and Caliban's Nature. . . . . Caliban represents (at present we must over-simplify) nature without benefit of nurture; Nature, opposed to an Art which is man's power over the created world and over himself; nature divorced from grace, or the senses without the mind. . . . .[2]

This statement leaves Ariel without function, and that is strange because Prospero is not a practical magician, in the play he is never instrumental in bringing about his own desires.

Robert Speaight in his most recent work, *Nature in Shakespearian Tragedy*, comes nearer than any other scholar to solving the problem of Ariel. In the chapter on *The Tempest*, he says:

> . . . . Thus Ariel may be said, further, to represent the Divine powers which are lent to his master. In one respect he is above Prospero, since he performs the things which Prospero cannot. In another respect, he is below him, since he obeys, for the time being, his behests. . . . .
>
> If Ariel is subject to Prospero, that is only because Prospero, through his mastery of magic, has borrowed the Divine prerogatives. It is as a priest and not as a man that Ariel obeys him. . . . .[3]

Here we have the first scholar to recognize clearly that Prospero cannot perform the acts he desires to take place. This is undeniably a gain in understanding; but I cannot agree that there is anything in the play that smacks of Christian doctrine. Grace and forgiveness were found in the religious cults and philosophic writings long before Paul wrote the Epistle to the Romans. The dialogues, *Phaedo* and *Tim-*

[2] *Ibid.*, pp. xxiv-xxv.
[3] *Loc. cit.*, pp. 156-7.

aeus, are devoted to the attributes of the soul. Is it not carrying interpretation a bit too far when Speaight says:

> Then he [Ariel] is the supernatural force at the service of man for the correction of human nature. Prospero uses him in a sacramental way, as the priest uses the bread and wine at Mass. . . . .[4]

I cannot agree with this notion of the play, and I doubt very much whether Shakespeare ever thought that human nature could be corrected.

My idea of the symbolism is as follows: Prospero is thought, and Ariel is the agent of the creative imagination, fulfilling the demands of Art. In Prospero, I find: intuition, thought, idea, form. Ariel is the executor and brings to fruition the desires of his master. Indeed, he is the one that gives shape to things. Prospero thinks—plans, but cannot practice. He needs a working agent to carry out his schemes. Hence, we have Ariel as the instrument of creative imagination—Art in action. To put it in terms of music, Prospero is the composer; Ariel, the performer.

When we think of the use of pen, pencil, musical notation, brush, chisel, we see form taking shape, and it is here we realize the hand is the servant of thought. Indeed, art is the child of mind and soul expressing form. Now, whether or not Shakespeare ever gave a thought to the symbolism of his play is to be doubted. Yet, it is there, I admit, and the student would miss a great deal if he did not realize it, or if he ignored it. It in no way helps the actor, and I do not think one in a thousand who witnesses a performance would imagine that it was a dramatic treatise on the mystery of the creative imagination.

I have never been able to understand what is meant by the opposition of Art to Nature. The timidity of the anti-pantheists cannot be excused. It is hard to explain the reason

[4] *Ibid.*, p. 157.

for their fears. Nature—the created universe, and all that therein is contained—was called the footstool of God by the Early Fathers. The stories of Jesus in the New Testament are chiefly nature stories. In the parables, the subjects are the fields, the grain, the birds of the air, and the lilies; and many are the references to those who till the land.

The nature in us, for good or evil, is not only the material for the philosopher, but for the poet, and they cannot work without it. Caliban is Nature, so is Prospero—magician though he is. He may have supernatural powers, but he cannot live without food and rest. The musician, the poet, the painter and the sculptor find their raw material in Nature and transmute it, by the crafts of Art, into things of beauty. Therefore, it seems to me that the idea of placing Nature and Art in two entirely different categories is to ignore the fact that Shakespeare never once divorced them. To him one was the complement of the other, and many times he tells us so:

> Yet nature is made better by no mean
> But nature makes that mean: so, over that art,
> Which you say adds to nature, is an art
> That nature makes. . . . .[5]

The perplexity of the scholars, in this respect, is probably brought about by a desire to explain away the real significance of Caliban in the play. They do not like nature in the raw when it is presented in a sub-human creature. Yet, Caliban in this play is as vital to its scheme as Ariel. It was genius at its apogee to conceive such a creature as a contrast to Prospero's enemies. And what the poet makes of him, when he comes in contact with the creatures of civilization, is one of the most severe contrasts we have in literature of any kind.

Thought without action—performance—is sterile in all forms of art. It serves the philosopher, as in the cases of Plato, Aristotle and Plotinus, but in drama it must be trans-

[5] *The Winter's Tale*, Act IV, scene 3.

muted and shaped into action to be acted and seen by the groundlings. Their instincts are not refined away by education. They are the sternest critics of our productions. Without the pit and gallery no play can succeed. The stalls cannot meet the expense today. In Shakespeare's time, the penny auditor's opinion of a play was of more value to the players than that of the few who sat in favored places.

Professor Reese, in his invaluable work, *Shakespeare, His World and His Work*, comes nearer to the Shakespearian idea of Nature than any of the experts. Referring to the Perdita-Polixenes scene in *The Winter's Tale*, he says:

> . . . . Shakespeare was here insisting that art, as the interpreter of Nature's laws and therefore a means whereby man may fulfil his proper function, often added to Nature by elucidating mysteries which life itself left dark. Art, in fact, was the finest of Nature's achievements: the shadow of life that was somehow more solid than the reality.[6]

The Tempest is the summing up of the thoughts that had burdened Shakespeare's soul since he was a young man. Those critics are right who emphasize that the plays indicate that the author held to the old ideas of an established order of economic freedom as a means to hours of leisure that could be given to the education of the mind and inspiration to the soul. It is inconceivable that any earnest student reading the histories of the English dynasties can ignore the fact that Shakespeare always held closely in mind the memory of happier days. Surely it cannot be doubted that he had learned of them not only from the tracts and pamphlets of the times, but also from the stories his grandfather must have told to his father.

The Tempest is a declaration for the restoration of the law and custom of the land. Let bygones be bygones, but restore. He knew his Bible. He knew the import of Isaiah's

[6] *Loc. cit.,* p. 494.

proclamation about "the repairer of the breach," the "restorer of paths to dwell in." It is a message of hope; perhaps the most earnest one the poet ever gave us. Reese says:

> . . . . Shakespeare never left man without hope, and the serenity of his final plays emerges from his strengthened conviction in an assured Providence which watches over men. Human experience is valid so far as it goes. Life is not just a general mist of error, nor the senses mere illusion: they speak truth to man, and possibly it is the only truth he may surely know. . . . .[7]

To this I can but say, "Amen."

[7] *Ibid.*, p. 453.

Eleven

THE TEMPEST
AS AUTOBIOGRAPHY

IT HAS BEEN assumed by several of the Shakespearian essay-
ists that Prospero is in some way a portrait of Shakespeare
himself. I can understand how they have reached that notion,
but a deep study of the play refutes it, because the hinter-
land of the author and the character he has created are entirely different; the wonder is that a likeness can be seen in
them.

Frank Kermode puts this matter before us clearly:

> . . . . It may be said that by the time Saintsbury
> wrote his chapter in the *Cambridge History* it had
> been accepted that *The Tempest* was a personal fare-
> well and a personal allegory. In the meantime the con-
> cept of the "final period" had gained universal support,
> and the authoritative view of this final stage of Shake-
> speare's development was given by Dowden, who
> described this period as being the result of Shake-
> speare's emergence from the depths of despair, the
> work of a mature and calm artist "On the Heights."[1]

This must refer to Prospero as he appears in the play. It
does not, however, take into consideration the totally different state of affairs experienced by Shakespeare before he
left London for the last time, nor does it take account of the
state of Milan before Prospero abdicated the dukedom.
There, we may take it, the state was governed justly, and

[1] *Loc. cit.*, pp. lxxxi-lxxxii.

108

the people were contented. When Miranda asks her father
why Antonio and his ministers did not destroy them, Prospero says:

> . . . . Dear, they durst not,
> So dear the love my people bore me; nor set
> A mark so bloody on the business; but
> With colours fairer painted their foul ends.[2]

It may be that Prospero was wise enough to rule as little
as possible, and to let the people attend to their own affairs.
Surely that would be an exceptional community. But it is
not at all surprising that a dire change could take place in the
fortunes of the people of Milan when bribed men gathered
round a usurper or a despot. This points to the historic undoing of a state that has known happy days. Egypt, Greece
and Rome are examples of such conspiracies that brought
them to a lingering death. Romaine Paterson's *The Nemesis
of Nations* tells in vivid prose the story of the fall of these
states.

Shakespeare's experience of men and their affairs is a
totally different one from that of Prospero. As I have tried
to make clear, his forebears had lived in the reigns of four
monarchs: Henry VIII, Edward VI, Mary, and Elizabeth.
The changes that took place in England during these reigns
were so extraordinary that scarcely anything that was for the
good of the people, as they had known it in the so-called
Golden Age, remained to give them hope of betterment.
Shakespeare knew the past. He had learned it from his
father; and as his grandfather, Richard, died only three years
before he was born, it may be assumed that the stories of
these three reigns before Elizabeth came to the throne were
fresh in the mind of his father.

The change that had taken place since the days when Sir
John Fortescue was Lord Chancellor, during the reign of

[2] *The Tempest*, Act I, scene 2.

Henry VI, cannot be appreciated by those critics who have overlooked or ignored the evidence of a better time, brought to an end by the Wars of the Roses. I have recently searched several histories, published during the nineteenth century, for an economic and political account of the condition of England before the coming of the Tudors. But in them I find only slight information of the sort that More gives us in *Utopia*.

The conservative view of things, in this connection, is misleading. The reader of the histories that I have looked into more than once lately will find very little about a "merrie England." But if he will turn to John Richard Green's *Short History of the English People*, in the section on "The New Monarchy, 1471-1509," he will find the following description of the power of the king and his parliament:

> . . . . The Wars of the Roses did far more than ruin one royal house or set up another on the throne. If they did not utterly destroy English freedom, they arrested its progress for more than a hundred years. They found England, in the words of Commines, "among all the world's lordships of which I have knowledge, that where the public weal is best ordered, and where least violence reigns over the people." A King of England—the shrewd observer noticed—"can undertake no enterprise of account without assembling his Parliament, which is a thing most wise and holy, and therefore are these Kings stronger and better served" than the despotic sovereigns of the Continent. The English kingship, as a judge, Sir John Fortescue, could boast when writing at this time, was not an absolute but a limited monarchy; the land was not a land where the will of the prince was itself the law, but where the prince could neither make laws nor impose taxes save by his subjects' consent. At no time had Parliament played so constant and prominent a part in the government of the realm. . . . .[3]

[3] P. 289.

Here, it is necessary to remark that Green has survived the adverse criticism of the court historians, and in the light of recent additions to our knowledge of the Plantagenet and Tudor dynasties, his work deserves the tribute paid to it by Stubbs. It is so superior in its description of the condition of the peasantry of that time that it may be studied afresh with advantage by scholars of this day. Read it again, for it is the work of a historian who wrote with no party bias.

What Henry Tudor could not get from Parliament, in the way of granting almost despotic rule to him, forced him to resort to the iniquitous Star Chamber. Then the liberty of the Commons suddenly disappeared and, as Green remarks, "The slow work of the age that went before was rapidly undone."

> . . . . So vast and sweeping was the change that to careless observers of a later day the constitutional monarchy of the Edwards and the Henries seemed suddenly to have transformed itself under the Tudors into a despotism as complete as the despotism of the Turk. . . . .[4]

Green thinks that this view of affairs may be exaggerated, but he maintains, nevertheless, that it is hard to connect the kingship of the old English Norman, Angevin, or Plantagenet kings "with the kingship of the House of York or of the House of Tudor."

What had been lost? I have presented the reader with the views of More, Hugh Latimer, Bernard Gilpin, and several other eye witnesses of the work of decay under the Tudors. That there had been something like a Golden Age in the fifteenth century may be inferred from the testimony to be found in Sir John Fortescue's work, *De Laudibus legum Angliae* (*In Praise of the Laws of England*):

> Neither doth the King there, either by himself or by his servants and officers, levy upon his subjects toll-

[4] *Ibid.*, p. 290.

ages, subsidies, or any other burdens, or alter their
laws or make new laws without the express consent
and agreement of his whole realm in his Parliament.
Wherefore every inhabiter of that realm useth and en-
joyeth at his pleasure all the labour of others, he gain-
eth by land or water. And hereby it cometh to pass
that the men of that land are rich, having abundance
of gold and silver, and other things necessary for the
maintenance of man's life. They drink no water unless
it be that some for devotion, and upon a zeal of
penance, do abstain from other drink. They eat plentifully of all kinds of flesh and fish. They wear fine
woollen cloth in their apparel. They have also abundance of bed coverings in their houses, and of all other
woollen stuff. They have great store of all hustlements
and implements of household. They are plentifully
furnished with all other things that are requisite to the
accomplishment of a quiet and wealthy life.[5]

The historians of the nineteenth century did not think
it worth while to quote this description of the state of England under Henry VI.

This disparity between the background of Prospero and
his creator makes all the difference in the world when we
consider the play autobiographically. If there be a similarity
at all, it must arise out of the events that happen in the play
after the curtain rises. The past of our author and the magician he has created are dissimilar in every respect. England,
in the lifetime of Shakespeare's known forebears, was totally
unlike the state of Milan when Prospero surrendered his
office to his brother Antonio. Yet, in a way, it may be assumed that one had experienced a Golden Age that was only
a history to the other.

Shakespeare knew the menace of the past was the cause
of the present turmoil. He knew that the evil that men do

[5] As quoted in Charles Plummer, *The Governance of England* (London, 1885), chap. III.

lives after them. Elizabeth had striven to correct abuses in religion, administration, monopolies, and other affairs which bore hardly upon her subjects. But her period was out of joint, and her efforts at reform had scarcely time to bring about a happier condition of affairs for the generality. It is true new vistas in trade and finance were opened up by the discovery of the New World. But even in Shakespeare's day Richard Hakluyt (who wrote *The Principal Navigations, Voyages, Traffics, and Discoveries of the English Nations,* which the English historian Froude called "The Prose Epic of the English Nation") had said that able men were gibbeted by the dozen.

I agree with Edward Dowden that in *The Tempest* Shakespeare rose from the depths of despair. That is the condition of his mind I have tried to emphasize. The plays of the last ten years of his life provide enough evidence to convince us that he survived hours of the deepest gloom. *Timon of Athens,* written three years before *The Tempest,* is the outpouring of a soul in anguish. This was a torrent of denunciation that had been pent up for years. He had to get it off his mind. The impotence of men to right wrongs, their strivings for power in the state, their detestable conspiracies against one another, their utter intolerance, their abject servility when it was necessary to gain their end, filled Shakespeare's soul with loathing, and in *Timon of Athens* he condemned the lot.

This period of despair could not have been caused by personal troubles, nor by domestic affliction. There is no record of his being in financial straits nor having to contend with business disagreements with his partners in the theater. He seemed to walk into a slough of despond when he was well-to-do. He had land and property and good friends. At home, in Stratford, Susanna and Judeth were happily married, and there we may be sure the atmosphere was bright and cheerful. There was every reason why he should have been content with his lot. A few lines spoken by Prospero give me the idea that he loved children:

> *Mir.* Alack, what trouble
> Was I then to you!
> *Pros.* O, a cherubin
> Thou wast that did preserve me. Thou didst smile,
> Infused with a fortitude from heaven,
> When I have deck'd the sea with drops full salt,
> Under my burthen groan'd; which rais'd in me
> An undergoing stomach, to bear up
> Against what should ensue.[6]

I can picture him looking into the face of a healthy child and seeing in it sincerity and joy.

It has been advanced by some of the critics that his despair was occasioned by the imprisonment of Southampton, but the Essex rebellion failed in 1601, and the Earl was executed on the 25th of February. Southampton was not released from prison until after the death of Elizabeth. This also raises the question about the nature of the friendship, or acquaintanceship, of the author of Venus and Adonis and the patron to whom he dedicated this poem.

The social acceptance of an actor-poet on a basis of friendship would have been unlikely, but a stage-struck youth, loving letters, in that day when the court and the aristocracy welcomed the New Learning, would certainly haunt the theater and the company of actors. All this is reasonable enough, but there is no evidence at all that a bond of friendship of any kind was forged. Dover Wilson says in *The Essential Shakespeare:*

> Accept the *Sonnets,* and we must believe that the nineteen-year-old Earl of Southampton, to whom as is now generally believed they were addressed, was the

[6] *The Tempest,* Act I, scene 2.

most splendid and captivating human being that Shakespeare had yet seen, and that he paid him the devotion of a whole heart. In that age of fulsome adulation, Shakespeare is a marvel of restraint and self-respect. . . . .[7]

More than that, the poet who wrote the plays was, above all, a manly man. Indeed, it might be said that both comedies and tragedies made their appeal in the strongest terms to masculine creatures. The virility of the fiber of his characters and the language they speak, whether they be good or bad people, is found in every piece he wrote. And who gave the chaste woman a brighter crown than he placed upon the heads of Imogen, Cordelia, and many other virtuous creations whom he seemed to glory in making known?

I cannot share the belief that Shakespeare's period of despair was brought about by the disaster that had fallen upon Southampton. About the time of his arrest, Shakespeare wrote *As You Like It* and *Twelfth Night*, and none would think that the author of these plays was plunged in gloom. When he wrote *Timon of Athens*, Southampton had been in prison for seven years. That would be a very long time for a busy playwright to mourn the loss of a friend. Therefore, I think we must count Southampton out as a cause for the year of spiritual depression.

It was not one single affair that was gnawing at his soul; it was an accumulation of historic events that had changed England. Many of the Shakespearian experts realize that in the mind of the poet, order held a high place. So far as his own life was concerned, he never stooped to a mean, irregular artifice to gain an advantage over anyone. It is one of the most astonishing things in the life of one we know so little about that there is no record of a misdemeanor or a quarrel with his fellows; of a failure to keep a promise or fulfill a

[7] P. 58.

contract. There are no blots upon the diary of his days, although it is true that Greene lampooned him scurvily and to such an extent that the publisher of the screed confessed his regret in having to do with its issue.

Twelve

MAGIC, WIZARDRY
AND WITCHCRAFT

So FAR, I have searched in vain for even the slightest similarity between the lives of Prospero and Shakespeare. Milan, up to the time when the duke chose to devote his life to his books, was so unlike the London of Elizabeth's day that it might have been a place removed from political strife.

However, perhaps the key to the parallel between poet and character may be found in a study of esoteric science. For a better understanding of many of the subtleties in the play we might consider this clue to the creation of Prospero.

The term "occult," of course, is scoffed at by the sophisticated, but our modern know-alls should remember that we are concerned with a period when educated people believed in witchcraft. The dictionary gives the following definition of the occult, which is of singular interest to us who are studying *The Tempest:*

> Dealing with, or in the arts, or practices involving the supposed action or influence of supernatural agencies, or some secret knowledge of them, as alchemy, magic, necromancy, astrology; also, relating to these arts; as, occult sciences or philosophers.

It is not only in this play that I find Shakespeare's mind running in this direction. Think of Prince Hamlet. He had been schooled at Wittenberg, where there were educated people who believed in the devil, and none more firmly than

Martin Luther himself. Although the play is set at a time long before Wittenberg knew the reforming priest, we may imagine that the faculty at the university was no more sophisticated than any other before the Reformation took place.

When Hamlet's mother asks: "Why seems it so particular with thee?" Hamlet replies, "I know not 'seems.' " He then goes on to tell her that his appearance in solemn black, his dejected behavior are appearances of grief,

> But I have that within which passeth show;
> These but the trappings and the suits of woe.[1]

"*That within*"—that which is not seen and which he will not reveal—is the potent matter that concerns him. Later on, after the visitation of the Ghost, he tells Horatio:

> There are more things in heaven and earth, Horatio,
> Than are dreamt of in your philosophy.[2]

Few grasp the significance of this mood of Hamlet. No critic I have read has followed this clue to his spiritual distress. Why did the poet place the "seems" speech—"that within"—in the first direct statement Hamlet utters? And this to his mother! There can be no doubt about the melancholy that enshrouds him. What, then, can "that within" be —the affliction which is more than grief for the loss of his father? Soul sorrow! caused by the realization of the impotence of man to dispel the woe of the world. "How weary, stale, flat, and unprofitable seem to me all the uses of this world." [3]

In London there were "things rank and gross in nature." The devil was abroad day and night, and the legions who worked for him—witches—were here, there and everywhere. Both high and low feared Walsingham's spies and

[1] Act I, scene 2.
[2] *Ibid.*, scene 5.
[3] *Ibid.*, scene 2.

Burleigh-bribed informers. People changed their religious belief to save their heads.

There was enough turmoil in everyday life to cause Shakespeare to create characters that would speak his inmost thoughts.

> . . . . The devil hath power
> To assume a pleasing shape, yea, and perhaps
> Out of my weakness and my melancholy—
> As he is very potent with such spirits—
> Abuses me to damn me. . . . .[4]

In *Macbeth*, both Banquo and the Thane of Glamis use words that indicate their desire to know more than their senses perceive; we are aware that a secret is hidden from them, which they cannot divine. Banquo says to the Witches:

> If you can look into the seeds of time,
> And say which grain will grow and which will not,
> Speak then to me. . . . .[5]

Macbeth cries,

> Stars, hide your fires!
> Let not light see my black and deep desires.[6]

Many other such expressions in the tragedies compel one to meditate upon the influences that often steer the mind of the poet to deal with the subtleties of the occult.

There is a definite cue to this in *The Tempest*. Prospero tells his daughter that his reputation was high for his knowledge of the liberal arts and that, when he cast the government upon his brother, he grew a stranger to his state, *"being transported and rapt in secret studies."*

The belief in magic is one of the oldest of superstitions. It antedates known religion. During the Christian era, many

---

[4] Act II, scene 2.
[5] *Macbeth*, Act I, scene 3.
[6] *Ibid.*, scene 4.

famous men not only gave it deep consideration but wrote about it. St. Augustine in his writings has much to say about sorcery. The author of the article on "Magic" in the *Cambridge Medieval History*[7] states that a contemporary of Augustine, Synesius of Cyrene, was a student of the occult and of divination. We learn from this essay that, in the ninth century, an archbishop wrote a book in which he attacked the belief in magic weather-making.

The bibliographies in recent encyclopedias and histories of works on magic run into the hundreds. Sir James Frazer and Dr. R. R. Marett in their works have devoted many chapters to the occult. So we wonder what it was that brought Shakespeare to the consideration of "secret studies," and why he should create a character who practiced magic. During the sixteenth century there were several works published in Europe, and particularly in Italy, on magic, alchemy and witchcraft, and it is not unreasonable to suggest that Shakespeare had heard about them and perhaps discussed them with men who taught Italian in London.

What works could he have read about magic, wizardry and witchcraft? The early plays indicate that he knew not a little about these subjects. This leads to another question: What books of this order would a cultivated gentleman in the sixteenth century have in his library? He certainly would have those which dealt with the burning questions of the day.

There were two works published a few years before Shakespeare was born which might have been found in the library of a manor. One was by Marsilio Ficino and the other by Marzio Galeotti. There was also another, written by a theologian known to be a famous magician, who was present at the Council of Pisa.

Agrippa von Nettesheim was one of the most versatile of all the learned men of that period. The work that brought

[7] Professor Lynn Thorndike, Vol. VIII, chap. XXII.

him into difficulties with abbots and monks was *De occulta philosophia*, written about 1510, but its publication was delayed until 1531. The monks accused him of believing in magic, and Agrippa's defense of a woman accused of witchcraft brought forth protests from the Inquisitor. His book upon the occult aroused storms of accusations against him from many of the monasteries, but his book went into many editions, and we may well imagine that it was in such a library as that of Sir Richard Newport at High Ercall.

I do not doubt that that library also contained the famous work *Malleus Maleficarum*, written by two Dominican Inquisitors, and first published at Cologne in 1489. This comprehensive treatise on witchcraft in all its phases had a very wide influence and went into at least four editions before the end of the fifteenth century. The authors were accredited by Pope Innocent VIII in his Bull of 1484.

From commentators upon this subject we learn that during the fifteenth and sixteenth centuries tracts and pamphlets came from the presses in quantities. The works published by churchmen during the fifteenth century run into the hundreds. There was no line drawn between magic and witchcraft that signified much to the masses, and so great was the belief of the folk in these arts, as they were called, that with all the crusading work done up to this day, there are still people just as superstitious as those of Shakespeare's time.

When I was a boy, old peasant women talked very gravely about witches, and in case a stranger were near, the remarks were carried in whispers. In the sixteenth century the devil was the personification and symbol of all dread and terror, but after the last witch was tried in England, in 1712, the craft was practiced under other labels.

The writers on magic often touch upon the magician's power to create storms at sea. In several of his dramas, Shakespeare has described the anger of the heavens. In *King Lear*, in *Othello*, and in *The Winter's Tale* his descriptions of Nature in a rage seem to indicate a passion for these disturbances. His vivid pictures of them startle us and give us pause, while we wonder if there is not something spiritual in the way that he treats these riots of the skies. Was, perhaps, the fury of a storm the counterpart of what went on within his own soul? In *The Winter's Tale*, the clown is telling the shepherd of the storm, and of it says, "Betwixt the firmament and it you cannot thrust a bodkin's point."

In *Othello* a gale is described in these phrases:

The chidden billow seems to pelt the clouds;
The wind-shak'd surge, with high and monstrous mane,
Seems to cast water on the burning bear. . . . .[8]

In *King Lear*, Kent says:

The tyranny of the open night's too rough
For nature to endure.[9]

Macbeth, in the Witches Scene, demands of the "secret, black, and midnight hags,"

I conjure you, by that which you profess,—
Howe'er you come to know it,—answer me:
Though you untie the winds and let them fight
Against the churches; though the yesty waves
Confound and swallow navigation up. . . . .[10]

Here are a few more examples of what the poet had in mind before he wrote his farewell play:

Blow, winds, and crack your cheeks! Rage! Blow!

Vaunt-couriers to oak-cleaving thunderbolts.

Crack Nature's moulds.

Since I was man
Such sheets of fire, such bursts of torrid thunder,

[8] Act II, scene 1.
[9] Act III, scene 4.
[10] *Macbeth*, Act IV, scene 1.

Such groans of roaring wind and rain, I never
Remembered to have heard.

From works upon witchcraft, magic, alchemy and necromancy we learn that the scholars of the Middle Ages treated
the black arts with grave consideration. A treatise on physical
science, written in the thirteenth century, contains the following:

> . . . . For Blessed Albertus Magnus in his work *De
> Passionibus aeris* says that rotten sage, if used as he ex-
> plains, and thrown into running water, will arouse
> most fearful tempests and storms.[11]

These are mere hints of how scholars who lived long before Shakespeare wrote *The Tempest* regarded storms. Consider this premonition of the storm that opens *The Tempest:*

Thou think'st 'tis much that this contentious storm
Invades us to the skin: so 'tis to thee;
But where the greater malady is fix'd,
The lesser is scarce felt. Thou'dst shun a bear;
But if thy flight lay toward the roaring sea,
Thou'dst meet the bear i' the mouth. When the mind's free
The body's delicate; the tempest in my mind
Doth from my senses take all feeling else
Save what beats there. . . . .[12]

"The tempest in my mind." Does that not mean the tempest was in the mind of the poet? Possibly in the tragedies
all the references to the turbulence of the elements have a
direct relation to the spiritual suffering of Shakespeare.

The storm, which is raging at the opening of *The Tempest,* is not an aggravation of Nature. It is totally different
from any other described by our poet. A magician has con-
jured it up for his own set purpose. Such power over the
elements seems superhuman, but it is a matter of great con-

---

[11] As quoted in *Malleus Maleficarum* (London: The Pushkin Press,
1948); first English trans., p. 12.
[12] *King Lear,* Act III, scene 4.

cern if we would understand Prospero, the human storm
god.

Some of the critics have treated the magical power of
Prospero superficially; others have ignored it completely.
Why this should be, I cannot make out. Here we have a
character quite different from any other Shakespeare ever
created—one who knows that the ship of Alonso has left
Africa and is on its way to Naples. Such omniscience would
indicate some form of telepathy. Hence, it is quite reasonable
for one to wonder if the King of Naples and Antonio were
thinking and speaking about the fate of Prospero during the
voyage.

Also, one wonders by what magical process did Prospero
learn about the conspiracy of Sebastian and Antonio to murder the King and Gonzalo?

It is unworthy of consideration by the people of this
sophisticated age to imagine that there were ever human
beings who occupied their minds with such nonsense. But
what people believe today and what they believed at the
time of Shakespeare makes all the difference in appreciating
the somewhat prophetic magical powers of Prospero in action.

The Reverend Montague Summers, in his introduction to
Malleus Maleficarum, presents us with a detailed story of
the belief in witchcraft and necromancy as it was practiced
for centuries before Shakespeare was born. Here is what
he has to say about the opinion of an authority who lived in
the sixteenth century:

> . . . . Jean Bodin, the famous jurisconsult (1530-90)
> whom Montaigne acclaims to be the highest literary
> genius of his time, and who, as a leading member of the
> Parlement de Paris, presided over important trials,
> gives it as his opinion that there existed, not only in
> France, a complete organization of witches, immensely
> wealthy, of almost infinite potentialities, most cleverly

captained, with centres and cells in every district, util-
izing an espionage in every land, with high-placed ad-
herents at court, with humble servitors in the cot-
tage. . . . .[13]

If that were the state of affairs in France, we know that
it must have been just as bad in England and Scotland when
James I succeeded Elizabeth.

One of the most interesting problems in this play concerns the power of Ariel to carry out the desires of his master.
Prospero is a human creature who, to move from one place
to another, must use his legs and feet. Ariel has wings. He
is not human. He can dart here and there, soar aloft, and set
the elements in a rage, lead people astray, into swamps and
briers, and can charm them with music and song.

This magical gift would have been accepted by the audience at the Globe without question. I doubt very much
whether courtier or groundling would have quibbled for a
moment over the matter of whether Prospero was a magician
practicing white magic or a necromancer who was evilly
disposed.

All this exposition is necessary, if we are to understand
the subtleties of *The Tempest*. There have been so many
different opinions voiced about the play, its author, the significance of the character of Prospero, his power as a magician,
and the utility of Ariel, that I think it important to give the
reader this all-too-brief sketch of the man who, in his dramatic works, never forgave foul play until he wrote the last one.

[13] P. xiii.

Thirteen

THE PROBLEM
OF STAGING THE PLAY

Now we shall leave the literary and philosophical analysis for the more practical matter of staging the play. The stage director who undertakes to produce a drama of Shakespeare finds the task quite as difficult as if he had to produce an unprinted work, a new one fresh from the hand of the author. This fact is not always appreciated by the scholars, for a copy of any of the plays can be bought for a small sum. Indeed, there are editions so cheap that one wonders how so much of intellectual and cultural value can be had for so little.

Nevertheless, the preparatory work required of the man who will have to mount the play and rehearse the actors entails as much labor as if it had never before been staged. He may know it thoroughly; perhaps he has seen it several times, but if he be an artist worth his salt, he will desire to interpret it in his own way. No matter how often the plays are staged, one performance differs from another, and the chief roles are portrayed with touches of characterization that others have not given to them.

After the director has digested thoroughly several new readings of the play, he will start to work upon what is called the prompt book. His first job will be to make a ground plan of the scenes, that is, indicating whether they be interiors or exteriors. He will also mark the exits and entrances, and the position of the properties, whether furniture or rocks, trees or bushes; indeed, whatever is essential for the actor's movement when he is upon the scene.

All this is a necessary preliminary and must be done before he can instruct the actor whether he enters a door right and walks to table center; or enters from the left second entrance and goes upstage and hides behind a bush.

The design of the scene—whether a room or an open heath—must be fully pictured by him, so that he can instruct the scenic artist and the men who make the properties. They must know what is called for, and it will be necessary for them to act conjointly in carrying out their work.

Then there are all the problems of costumes, wigs, armor and other properties which the actors and actresses will wear and handle. When all this work is thought out, the stage director will take the ground plan of each scene and mark upon it the essential movements of the players. Briefly, this is what the stage director should do before the first rehearsal.

The printed copy of the play will be of no use to the actors, for the directions to be inserted will be so elaborate that there would not be room upon the page to write them in. Therefore, parts will have to be made from the prompt book, which describe the essential movements of each player. The ideal method of rehearsal is for the first one to take place in a scene that will be presented to the audience, with all the properties in place.

I remember only one production that began in this way, and that was a revival of *Romeo and Juliet* at the Hof-Theater in Munich. Probably such a method is now carried out at the Memorial Theatre at Stratford. I do not know, but I can say that I have seen three great productions of the plays by well-known actors, when the scenes were not set until a few days before the curtain rose upon the first performance.

It is well for the reader to know something about the

preparatory work of the stage director, for we are going to
consider *The Tempest* as a play to be given in a theater
before an audience. Perhaps this sketchy statement will help
us in following some rather intricate scenes in the printed
play, which are bare of any suggestion about what certain
characters are doing on the stage while others are in action.
There are several of this order.

Now let us prepare the play for the first rehearsal. A ship
is laboring in a tempest of thunder and lightning. The captain tells the boatswain to urge the sailors to act smartly
or the vessel will run aground. We know not the port she
has left nor her destination. The situation is desperate; an
order is given to take in the topsail and pay attention to the
master's whistle. The passengers then come up on the deck.
They are Alonso, Sebastian, Antonio, Ferdinand, Gonzalo,
and others. The first tells the boatswain to be careful and
asks for the master. They are ordered to go below at once,
and keep their cabins. The boatswain reminds them that the
roaring waves do not care for the name of King, but Gonzalo tells him to remember whom he has on board.

In their despair, they seek their cabins again and leave
the crew to handle the vessel as best they can. Perhaps another great lurch of the ship sends Sebastian, Antonio and
Gonzalo on deck again. We know not who the passengers
are, but the crew seem to know that one is a King.

When the boatswain sees them, he cries:

> Yet again! what do you here? Shall we give o'er,
> and drown? Have you a mind to sink?[1]

Their terror is shown in the epithets that they cast at
the sailor:

> *Seb.* A pox o' your throat, you bawling, blasphem-
> ous, incharitable dog!
> *Boats.* Work you, then.

[1] The quotations in this chapter are taken from Act I of the play,
unless otherwise noted.

Ant. Hang, cur! hang, you whoreson, insolent noise-
maker. We are less afraid to be drowned than thou
art.

Gon. I'll warrant him for drowning, though the
ship were no stronger than a nutshell, and as leaky as
an unstanched wench.

Boats. Lay her a-hold, a-hold! set her two courses;
off to sea again; lay her off.

The sailors rush upon the deck and declare all is lost and
that it is time to pray. Gonzalo tells the boatswain that the
King and Prince are at prayers. There is great agitation and
distress, while Antonio cries, "Let's all sink wi' th' King."
He and Sebastian leave the deck, and Gonzalo brings the
scene to an end saying:

Now would I give a thousand furlongs of sea for
an acre of barren ground, long heath, broom, furze,
anything. The wills above be done! but I would fain
die a dry death.

In this short scene, our curiosity is aroused concerning
the passengers, but of their identity we know only that one
is a King and that Gonzalo is a councellor. Yet, we are satisfied that the crew know who they are. We may take it that
the ship has run aground, that she is in danger of foundering
because she has split. The craftsmanship of the true dramatist
is revealed in this opening scene, for we glean enough from
it to know the vessel carries a royal personage and his retinue,
but not enough to know their fate.

This is a difficult set to stage. I have seen the piece produced in the theater and also in the open air at Regent's
Park. But at these performances scarcely any attempt was
made to give a realistic touch to the motion of the vessel in
a storm. Indeed, that was impossible at the open-air performance of the piece. Yet, to my knowledge, in melodramas
ship scenes have been staged with some attempt at realism.

I was once assistant stage manager of a production that

called for a storm-tossed vessel to strike an iceberg. The deck was placed on rockers, a false stage, and it was worked by the scene-shifters to lurch from side to side. As a bit of stage mechanism, it proved so effective that some of the audience suffered the symptoms of seasickness. The play was an utter failure.

Perhaps it is better to leave all this to the imagination of the spectator. We may be quite sure that at the Globe or even when the play was presented at Court, no attempt was made to show the motion of a ship in a storm.

This is not a matter of great concern. The difficulties that Bottom encountered in *A Midsummer Night's Dream* crop up now and then for modern stage managers to overcome, but Shakespeare himself was not loath to leave such problems to the imagination of his audience.

From the storm, the scene suddenly changes to an open space before the cell of Prospero. Before the design of this set can be made, the director must take into consideration the requirements of the action in other scenes, for the same set is used in the third, fourth and fifth acts.

The instruction reads merely: "The Island. Before Prospero's Cell." This is the bare suggestion. Therefore, the full picture must be created by the producer. He has to determine the topography and the herbaceous nature of the spot. He has to devise the entrances and the position of the cell.

The first characters to come upon the scene are Prospero and Miranda, who enter from the second entrance right. They have seen the wreck of the ship, and it is not likely they have made their way from that side of the stage where the cell is placed. They must have come from the shore.

The scene is a rocky part of the island, lying in a dell, which shows signs of having been cultivated. It may be arranged to have the entrance to the cell on the actors' left, in the second entrance. On the right, the landscape may open up and show, in the distance, cliffs shelving **down to the sea.**

At the back of the scene there are signs of land being cultivated and a grassy bank shaded by trees, hillocks and shrubs.

The cell is in a large rock set obliquely in the second
entrance, a natural cavern in which there is a hole high and
wide enough to admit a tall man. Nearby is a rude bench,
and behind it there is a line of rope or cord which hangs
from the rock to a tree. The storm has abated, but dark
clouds are moving swiftly. There should be rumblings of
distant thunder and occasional faint flashes of lightning. All
these will heighten the effect of Miranda's first speech.

When the lights are up, Prospero enters with Miranda.
He is wearing his magic robe. He tries to calm his daughter's
fears for the shipwrecked men, assuring her that no harm has
been done to the vessel in the storm. He asks her to assist
him in taking off his magic garment, which is laid upon the
bench near the cave. In placing it there, Prospero says, "Lie
there, my Art." He bids Miranda to sit down. Where? Upon
the bench? No, that cannot be, for in a little while she has
to fall into a long sleep.

The place where she reclines should be a sheltered bank
at the foot of a hillock, right center. For while she sleeps,
there is a long scene to be played. After she is seated, Prospero tells her the story of how and why he comes to be with
her on the island upon which they have spent twelve years.
Miranda was only three years old when they arrived there.

We learn that Prospero was the Duke of Milan, and his
coming to the island was the story of foul play. Miranda
rises and asks:

> What foul play had we, that we came from thence?
> Or blessed was't we did?

He replies,

>   Both, both, my girl:
> By foul play, as thou say'st, were we heav'd thence,
> But blessedly holp hither.

Prospero then tells the story of how he became an exile. His brother, Antonio, whom he loved, was left to manage the state while Prospero devoted himself to the study of the liberal arts. He cast the government upon Antonio because, owing to being "rapt in secret studies," he became a stranger to the state. Prospero says for him his "library was dukedom large enough." However, a conspiracy was formed against him, and his brother and the King of Naples sought a way to get rid of him. He and his daughter were hurried aboard the rotten carcass of a boat and left to their fate. But it had been well stocked by Gonzalo, a noble Neapolitan, who secretly, it is presumed, stored the ship with food, fresh water, "rich garments, linens, stuffs, and necessaries." Besides these goods,

> Knowing I lov'd my books, he [Gonzalo] furnish'd me,
> From mine own library with volumes that
> I prize above my dukedom.

After this account of his expulsion from Milan, he dons his mantle again, and Miranda asks him why he raised the sea storm. He replies that by a strange accident, "Fortune hath mine enemies brought to this shore." Miranda, evidently tired out from witnessing the shipwreck, shows fatigue, and Prospero tells her to sleep. When her eyes are closed, Prospero calls Ariel to him.

This character is unique. There is not one like Ariel in the plays. Even Puck himself in *A Midsummer Night's Dream* suffers by comparison, for the prowess of Ariel seems to be without limit, and the feats he performs are always miraculous. He has come from the ship and describes what has taken place. He has seen all the crew and passengers:

> Not a hair perish'd;
> On their sustaining garments not a blemish,
> But fresher than before: and, as thou bad'st me,
> In troops I have dispers'd them 'bout the isle.
> The King's son have I landed by himself.

The ship is safely in the harbor. Having carried out the orders of Prospero, Ariel reminds him that he has been promised his liberty. The time is not yet, for Prospero has much more for Ariel to perform, and becoming impatient with Ariel's desire for freedom, he reminds him how the foul witch Sycorax was banished to this island with Ariel, then her servant. The witch brought to the island with child was left there by sailors. Then we learn how Prospero found Ariel and used him as the agent of his art.

> *Pros.* . . . . Thou was a spirit too delicate
> To act her earthy and abhorr'd commands,
> Refusing her grand hests, she did confine thee,
> By help of her more potent ministers,
> And in her most unmitigable rage,
> Into a cloven pine; within which rift
> Imprison'd thou didst painfully remain
> A dozen years; within which space she died
> And left thee there, where thou didst vent thy groans
> As fast as mill-wheels strike. Then was this island—
> Save for the son that she did litter here,
> A freckled whelp hag-born, not honour'd with
> A human shape.
> *Ari.* Yes, Caliban her son.

Many of the ideas in this play give me the impression that Shakespeare might have heard from someone the stories found in Hesiod. Fifty years ago I presented this notion to two well-known Greek scholars, one of whom was George Brown, who assisted the learned Gilbert Murray in teaching Greek in Glasgow. Both scoffed at the idea. An edition of the works of Greek didactic poetry was published in Milan in 1493, but I can find no trace of *Works and Days* or the *Theogony* being known in England when Shakespeare lived.

In Hesiod there are many passages that have reference to the spirits of trees. Of course, there is a difference between the imprisonment of Ariel in a cloven pine and the hama-dryads of Hesiod, who were the spirits of oaks and lived as long as the trees. But such an idea might have been distorted for dramatic purposes. Whether this be so or not, there are other scenes and passages in this play which seem to hark back to Hesiod. These will be dealt with as the scenes are considered.

The almost interminable discussions of the experts about the blue-eyed hag Sycorax have not led to a solution of the problem of her origin and activity, except that she was born in Argier. It is a fascinating study because it is all part and parcel of black magic. The one opinion about her, generally conceded, is that she is the symbol of the sub-human. Hence, Caliban, her son (an anagram of the word cannibal).

This latter creature is so wholly unlike anything Shakespeare imagined in the form of beast or man that we wonder at first why such a hideous thing should be used. But we soon learn that Caliban is an essential link in the drama. It is impossible to think of the scheme of *The Tempest* without him. He is the indispensable contrast, which is necessary for exposing the depths of infamy to which educated beings can fall.

I do not think anything can be gained by having recourse to the stories of the sea rovers and the imperial pirates (who followed the Spaniards to the New World) to establish a source from which Shakespeare drew this creature. Nor do I think it is permissible to lay stress upon a newly discovered island as the locale of this scene. I hope to show there are other sources for such an idea, which are found in classical literature. Still, we have to deal with Caliban as he is, and the story of his birth and upbringing as we hear it from Prospero.

When he appears, he puts a curse upon his master, who, in turn, threatens him with all kinds of torments. Then Caliban relates how Prospero treated him when he first came to the island. He asserts that, when he was alone, he was his own King and now—

 . . . . Here you sty me
In this hard rock, whiles you do keep from me
The rest o' th' island.

The significance of this declaration seems to be lost upon
most of our critics. Whether it be the education he has received from Prospero, or, on the other hand, a notion of first-
come first-served (which is no primitive idea), it certainly
indicates that the sense of proprietorship is a very old one;
and that, in this respect, the modern landlord differs little
from an aborigine.

But Prospero was a good landlord, and lodged this creature
in his own cell till he sought to violate the honor of his child.
Caliban's reply is a natural one:

O ho, O ho! would 't had been done!
Thou didst prevent me; I had peopled else
This isle with Calibans.

This takes us back to an idea of marriage before there
were such rites as civil and religious ceremonies.

In this scene Shakespeare might have been predicting the
imperial pitfalls of our own time. Prospero reminds Caliban
how he has been educated, and the latter replies:

You taught me language; and my profit on 't
Is, I know how to curse. The red plague rid you
For learning me your language!

In our own day, we have gone into Africa, Polynesia,
other countries of the Equator, and have taught the natives
our language. They aspire to be pupils in our colleges and
universities, and when they have learned their lessons, they
return home to become a thorn in the flesh of our administra-
tors. Imperialism, in the territorial sense, ultimately has its
own reward, and we should not be surprised when the natives
revolt.

Prospero orders Caliban to get to work, and threatens him
with pains and aches that will make him roar. However, the

education he has received has enlightened him about the wisdom of biding his time and, in an aside, he says:

> . . . . I must obey: his Art is of such pow'r,
> It would control my dam's god, Setebos,
> And make a vassal of him.

At this point in the drama it becomes necessary to reread the whole scene in order to learn what is the real grievance of Caliban against Prospero. To my mind it is of peculiar importance to the evolution of the play, for it is not improbable that Shakespeare had in mind the territorial adventures of Spanish navigators and the British imperialists who tracked them down and wrested their golden domains from them.

Caliban has told his master, "I am all the subjects that you have, which first was mine own King." The inference is that the island was deserted when the sailors abandoned Sycorax to give birth to her son. If this be the correct interpretation of the lines, we should have no difficulty in understanding the resentment of Caliban. This notion is supported by the prior statement in the same speech, in which he says:

> This island's mine, by Sycorax my mother,
> Which thou tak'st from me. . . . .

Frank Kermode, in his introduction to the play, gives us a very interesting account of what he calls "News from the New World," in which he discusses allegorical voyages, colonial adventures, and natives versus civilized people. But in my opinion he does not come to grips with the matter of Caliban's deep-seated grudge against Prospero, as discussed in a previous chapter.[2]

We sometimes forget that imperialism is a very old system of exploitation. There was nothing new in the methods used by the navigators of the Tudor period or, indeed, in those of the Victorian. All bore the same marks and misfortunes.

---

[2] *Supra*, chap. VIII.

In one respect only does the modern differ from the Tudor and the ancient, and that is in the intelligent administration, which was introduced in India by Sir Henry Maine and Elphinstone.

Of course, it is no easy task for men of this generation to ascertain exactly what did take place when the European Prosperos descended upon the natives of the Old and New Worlds. It is one thing to read the records but quite another to visit the places and see with one's own eyes the remnants of treasures that attracted them thence. It is a grave mistake to assume, as some of our critics do, that the lands of the Western world were isles of luxuriant vegetation and simple-minded natives. Surely the story of Pizarro refutes such notions of the overthrow and subjection of uncultured natives on islands containing no natural stores of precious minerals.

When one sees some of the trophies of the cultures destroyed by the Spaniards, one forms an entirely different conception of what attracted European adventurers to cross the Atlantic. When I was in Peru in 1939, I was taken to the Inca Museum to view the great finds that had recently been made at Cuzco. Although the exhibition was not yet open to the public, there were displays of the most beautiful gold and silver articles, wonderful domestic and ornamental pottery, and rich tapestries as bright in color as the day they were woven. Nothing I have seen in the museums of Spain surpassed in beauty and richness the work of the Inca. All this indicates that a culture of high art and living splendor was destroyed by Christian vandals.

The story of Cortez in Mexico is at variance with that told in *Purchas his Pilgrimage* (1613), one of the books quoted by Frank Kermode. The culture of the Mayans has often been compared with that of the Egyptians in the finest period of their history.

Therefore, we may accept the island, which Caliban claimed to be his, as it is given to us by the poet in his play.

Indeed, if we do so and do not bother about the stories of the sea rovers, we shall appreciate all the more the working out of the plot and the inevitable climax to be reached. The exploits of the conquistadores of the first half of the sixteenth century have nothing to do with *The Tempest*. That should be obvious to anyone who has read the play closely, for none of the characters had the slightest intention of going to the island. Not even Sycorax herself dreamed of such a visit until she was put ashore by the sailors.

We now make the acquaintance of one of the passengers of the wrecked ship, Ferdinand, the son of the King of Naples. Ariel, playing and singing, brings him onto the scene. When Miranda sees him, she is enthralled, and tells her father:

> I might call him
> A thing divine; for nothing natural
> I ever saw so noble.

This meeting has been brought about by Ariel, and so pleased is Prospero at what has been accomplished that he decides to set him free within two days. This is a most extraordinary case of love at first sight, for Ferdinand exclaims when he sees Miranda, "O you wonder! If you be maid or no." He is amazed to find that she speaks his language. The attraction of one for the other proceeds so rapidly that Prospero becomes alarmed and says to himself:

> They are both in either's pow'rs; but this swift business
> I must uneasy make, lest too light winning
> Make the prize light.

The ruse taken by Prospero to check the ardor of the lovers seems to be unduly severe. But it serves to bring to our notice the courage of Ferdinand and his readiness to assert his honor. Prospero accuses him of being a spy, and carries the test to extremes. When Miranda intervenes and says, "I'll be his surety," he then turns upon her in feigned anger, and the scene closes with the following:

Pros. Silence! one word more
Shall make me chide thee, if not hate thee. What!
An advocate for an impostor! hush!
Thou think'st there is no more such shapes as he,
Having seen but him and Caliban: foolish wench!
To th' most of men this is a Caliban,
And they to him are angels.
    Mir. My affections
Are then most humble; I have no ambition
To see a goodlier man.
    Pros. Come on; obey:
Thy nerves are in their infancy again,
And have no vigour in them.
    Fer. So they are:
My spirits, as in a dream, are all bound up.
My father's loss, the weakness which I feel,
The wrack of all my friends, nor this man's threats,
To whom I am subdued, are but light to me,
Might I but through my prison once a day
Behold this maid: all corners else o' th' earth
Let liberty make use of; space enough
Have I in such a prison.
    Pros. [*Aside*] It works. [*To Fer.*] Come on.
[*To Ariel*] Thou hast done well, fine Ariel! Follow me;
Hark what thou else shalt do me.
    Mir. Be of comfort;
My father's of a better nature, sir,
Than he appears by speech: this is unwonted
Which now came from him.
    Pros. Thou shalt be as free
As mountain winds: but then exactly do
All points of my command.
    Ari. To th' syllable.
    Pros. Come, follow. Speak not for him.

Prospero is satisfied with his cruel test of the manliness of Ferdinand, and compliments Ariel upon his share in bringing Ferdinand and Miranda together. The denunciation of Ferdinand has not affected her belief in him in any way.

It is a curious scene and not like any one in the other plays. It serves to bring out forcibly three special points of the drama: (1) the paternal desire to know that his daughter has met a man worthy of her; (2) the test of the suitor and the placing of a just estimate upon his nobility; (3) the end of the servitude of Ariel, which is a very important point. When Prospero promises that he will be "as free as mountain winds" our interest in this association is heightened and we wonder what extraordinary event is yet to come that will set him at liberty.

In this scene Shakespeare makes demands upon the actor that call for the fullest capability of his art. He has to play two conflicting roles: one, to assume an anger that he in no way feels; the other, to act the part of a parent delighted with the match she has made. To feign anger so that it will have its effect and, at the same time, suppress the joy of having accomplished a sweet desire is a task for any Prospero. But this is not all. Ariel is present, and Prospero turns to him twice in this scene, assuming at once his normal mood. These rapid changes of temper are enough to test the power of any actor. It is a difficult scene to play, and I must confess I cannot remember ever seeing a satisfactory performance of it.

Fourteen

ACT TWO—THE PLOTTERS

W E ARE NOW TAKEN to another part of the island and are introduced to the rest of the passengers of the ship. The glimpse we had of them at the opening of the play revealed that one was a king. Now we see them dressed according to the court custom of Milan and Naples. Their clothes have suffered no damage from the storm, owing to the charms exercised by Ariel.

The first to speak is Gonzalo, who is a councellor to Alonso, the King of Naples. He strives to soothe his friends by reminding them how fortunate they have been in saving their lives. But Antonio, the brother of Prospero, and Sebastian, the brother of the King, deride the good intentions of Gonzalo and ridicule his ponderous expressions.

These people have been to Tunis, attending the marriage of Alonso's daughter, Claribel, to the King. It is on their way back to Naples that the storm raised by Prospero has overtaken them and driven their ship ashore. Alonso mourns the loss of his son Ferdinand, but one of the courtiers, Francisco, saw him swim ashore, and he does not doubt that he survived. However, the King has lost hope and believes that he is gone. Sebastian upbraids him for wedding his daughter to the King of Tunis. They are all enduring nervous anxiety at high tension, and the play of words and badinage that pass are indicative of their plight.

Gonzalo tries in vain to cheer them up and, as a last resort, he turns the subject to the order of the island on which they find themselves. He says:

> Had I plantation of this isle, my lord—. . . .
> And were the King on 't, what would I do?[1]

He then describes, almost word for word, the conditions that reigned in the Isles of the Blest. The substance of the scheme of Gonzalo will be found in parts of the first section of *Works and Days*. We are reminded, also, of the Hyperboreans referred to by Herodotus. They lived in a paradise protected by the north wind, where there were perpetual sunshine and great fertility. Its people were free from disease and war, and they lived a thousand years. The dream of such an Elysium was in the minds of generation after generation of the Greeks. How Shakespeare came to know of it is a mystery, but the fitness of the notion, as it arises in this scene, cannot be questioned.

The Hyperboreans were vegetarians, and up to this point we have heard nothing of cattle or wild animals on the island. The Shakespearian experts have treated this scene far too lightly. Indeed, to my mind, it is the revelation of an economic order, which was a fundamental notion of our poet. Gonzalo says:

> *Gon.* All things in common Nature should produce
> Without sweat or endeavour: treason, felony,
> Sword, pike, knife, gun, or need of any engine,
> Would I not have; but Nature should bring forth,
> Of its own kind, all foison, all abundance,
> To feed my innocent people.
> *Seb.* No marrying 'mong his subjects?
> *Ant.* None, man; all idle; whores and knaves.
> *Gon.* I would with such perfection govern, sir,
> T' excel the Golden Age.

---

[1] The quotations in this chapter are from Act II, unless otherwise noted.

The idea of an economic order in which "Nature should bring forth, of its own kind, all foison, all abundance, to feed my innocent people" must have been a dream of many people in England after the Tudors came to the throne. For there had been a Golden Age of sorts, even when there were serfs. It is on record that such a one had several acres and a hut for which he paid a few days' labor or some simple product to the lord of the manor.

Suddenly Ariel, unseen, is heard playing solemn music, which induces drowsiness on all but Sebastian and Antonio. They wonder at what has fallen upon their companions, for they are not disposed to slumber, and admit that their spirits are nimble. Then, while the others are asleep, these two plot to murder Alonso and Gonzalo.

Assuring themselves that Ferdinand is drowned, they discuss the question of who is heir to the throne of Naples. The daughter of the King, Claribel, is in Tunis, and they count her out. Sebastian has been the instigator in this plot, but he has not found it hard to convince Antonio that by carrying it out, both would gain thrones. Antonio says:

> *Ant.* . . . . Here lies your brother,
> No better than the earth he lies upon,
> If he were that which now he's like, that's dead;
> Whom I, with this obedient steel, three inches of it,
> Can lay to bed for ever; whiles you, doing thus,
> To the perpetual wink for aye might put
> This ancient morsel, this Sir Prudence, who
> Should not upbraid our course. For all the rest,
> They'll take suggestion as a cat laps milk;
> They'll tell the clock to any business that
> We say befits the hour.
> *Seb.* Thy case, dear friend,
> Shall be my precedent; as thou got'st Milan,
> I'll come by Naples. Draw thy sword: one stroke
> Shall free thee from the tribute which thou payest;
> And I the King shall love thee.

> *Ant.* Draw together;
> And when I rear my hand, do you the like,
> To fall it on Gonzalo.

Sebastian and Antonio are no sons of Sycorax. They are educated gentlemen of high rank. One is the brother of the man to be murdered in his sleep; the other is the brother of Prospero. Here we have a full dose of conspiracy, regicide, and usurpation. All these crimes are dealt with in the other plays.

From what we know of Caliban, education has done little to curb his raw instincts. Twelve years under the guidance of Prospero and Miranda have not raised him above the level of the beast. The grudge he bears his master is a natural one. But the plot contrived by Antonio and Sebastian to murder Alonso and Gonzalo is an unnatural one. Here is one of the most vivid contrasts that Shakespeare has devised.

Neither trusts the other; they must act together. Then when the swords are out, ready for the kill, there is still something more to be agreed upon. At that moment Ariel, unseen, comes with music and a song, and into Gonzalo's ear whispers a warning. She sings:

> While you here do snoring lie,
> Open-ey'd conspiracy
> 　　His time doth take.
> If of life you keep a care,
> Shake off slumber, and beware:
> 　　Awake, Awake!

When the conspirators have discussed the last point to be decided and are ready for the attack, Gonzalo is aroused and cries, "Now, good angels, preserve the King." At that moment Alonso awakes and sees Sebastian and Antonio with their swords drawn. The cowards who would murder men in their sleep, fearing detection, invent a story of a "burst of bellowing like bulls, or rather lions." And Antonio says,

" 'Twas a din to fright a monster's ear, to make an earth-quake! sure, it was the roar of a whole herd of lions."

The story in which the liars take refuge has its effect. They all draw their weapons, with the object of making a search for Ferdinand. And they depart. Ariel then speaks:

> Prospero my lord shall know what I have done:
> So, King, go safely on, seek thy son.

And with this the scene closes.

In another part of the island we see Caliban carrying a burden of logs. And in a soliloquy he gives an account of all the tortures Prospero inflicts upon him from time to time. He regards every mere accident as part of his master's desire to punish him. And while he is in this mood, Trinculo, the King's jester, appears. Caliban looks upon him as a spirit come to torment him for bringing the wood in slowly; and, thinking he will not be noticed, falls flat upon the ground.

There is a storm brewing. Thunder is heard, and Trinculo fears it may break upon him. Seeing the prone figure of Caliban, he wonders if it is dead or alive, a man or a fish. The thunder becoming louder, Trinculo decides to creep under the cloak of Caliban for shelter.

Then enters Stephano, a butler, a bottle in his hand, singing a drunken song:

> The master, the swabber, the boatswain, and I,
>   The gunner, and his mate,
> Lov'd Mall, Meg, and Marian, and Margery,
>   But none of us car'd for Kate:
>   For she had a tongue with a tang,
>   Would cry to a sailor, Go hang!
> She lov'd not the savour of tar nor of pitch;
>   Yet a tailor might scratch her where'er she did itch.
>   Then to sea, boys, and let her go hang!

In passing, I may remark that Shakespeare knew the chanteys of the time. In this scene of low comedy (as it would have been called in the old days of melodrama) we are aware that Shakespeare drew upon his recollection of nights spent in the inns of the country. We think of Mistress Quickly, Doll Tearsheet, Pistol, Nym and Bardolph, the drunken revelry of demobilized soldiers and sailors, just ashore from voyages with the sea rovers. Such scenes lingered in his memory long after he had attained a position of eminence and wrote in the quiet of the gardens of the Stratford houses.

The wine that Stephano gives to Caliban in this scene is the first he has tasted and, as it sets his blood tingling, he cries with delight, "Hast thou not dropp'd from heaven?" He adores Stephano and promises to show him every fertile inch of the island. He is ready to kiss his foot and asks him to be his god. Trinculo has the wit to realize the havoc that has been wrought by the contents of Stephano's bottle, and says, "the poor monster's in drink. An abominable monster!"

Then from Caliban we hear something about the food yielded by Nature on the island. He will show Stephano where there are crabs, pig-nuts, nimble marmosets, clustering filberts, and young scamels. So fair is the prospect that Stephano cries out:

> I prithee now, lead the way, without any more talking. Trinculo, the King and all our company else being drown'd, we will inherit here: here; bear my bottle: fellow Trinculo, we'll fill him by and by again.

It is a splendid piece of irony on the part of the poet to make the drunken Caliban think he is to be rid of Prospero. He cries, "Farewell, master; farewell, farewell!" Then he sings a verse:

> No more dams I'll make for fish;
>   Nor fetch in firing
>   At requiring;
> Nor scrape trenchering, nor wash dish:

> 'Ban, 'Ban, Cacaliban
> Has a new master:—get a new man.

Alas, we know now only too well what alcohol has done to bring wild men under the heel of educated conquerors. In this scene the poet has shown the effect of liquor upon a sub-human creature. It has given him the semblance of courage to desert Prospero and become the slave of Stephano, who has the desire to inherit the island. The lust for power is in the drunken butler.

But in the scene that precedes this, Sebastian and Antonio were not drunk. They were quite sober when they conspired to murder Alonso and Gonzalo. Who else but Shakespeare could make us conscious of the depths to which human depravity could descend?

When we read scenes such as I have just described, we should be glad that Mrs. Grundy was not the spouse of the Lord Chamberlain in Elizabeth's day. Had she been in power we would have lost much, for she would have insisted upon toning down some of the bawdy and rough expressions and frowned upon the notion of a butler so forgetting his position (even in such a time of stress) as to lower himself to the position of a common drunkard.

Shakespeare was not bothered with people who would put a lacy nightgown upon flesh, showing blemishes of evil indulgences. He knew the parts that the Malls, the Megs, the Marians and the Margerys play in the lives of the roughneck denizens of the wharves. This is not to say that his courage should receive a compliment for describing them as he knew them—even in a chantey. He was a realist through and through, and never dreamed of toning down the character and speech of those whose lives are spent in the lower depths. We marvel at the scope of his experience of personages in high and low society. And our wonder increases mightily that he could observe so keenly and never descend to the level of these creatures. It is only the actor who can fully appreciate the searching examination of such people as Trinculo and Stephano.

To read this scene with the book upon the knee, in the quiet of the library, is a completely different experience from that of presenting these characters to an audience. The actor who plays Stephano must know a drunken man in nearly all his moods. His face, his lungs, his gorge, his limbs are all brought into play. With Caliban, the actor must show what is not indicated in the printed book—the effect of the first draught of wine transforming him from a sober creature to an exhilarated being. This scene impresses us with the fact that Shakespeare had the true investigator's eye, and what he observed in his early years was indelibly inscribed upon his mind.

Fifteen

ACT THREE—IDYLLIC
LOVE AND COURTSHIP

F ERDINAND HAS BEEN set to work. He enters, bearing a log for the fuel pile, but his labor is sweetened by the thought of Miranda. While we listen to his plaint about his tasks, Miranda enters. Her father is present but unseen during passages between the lovers, which for pure sentiment surpass anything that Shakespeare has written. She pities him for the labor he must undergo and would take the log from him and place it on the pile. He cannot resist the temptation of lingering with her, and is induced to stay awhile, for she tells him that her father is at his studies and that Ferdinand may rest safely for some three hours.

He confesses that he has known other women and found them wanting:

> . . . . For several virtues
> Have I lik'd several women; never any
> With so full soul, but some defect in her
> Did quarrel with the noblest grace she ow'd,
> And put it to the foil: but you, O you,
> So perfect and so peerless, are created
> Of every creature's best![1]

They do not embrace, nor does he imprint a kiss upon her cheek. It is simple adoration without any manifestation of amorous desire. When it is played in accordance with the

[1] The quotations in this chapter are taken from Act III of the play.

149

simplicity of the lines, we cannot help but feel there is something ethereal about it, and that the magician who is present,
but unseen, must rejoice that Ferdinand is worthy of his
child. There is not even a suggestion of a religious ceremony,
and in this respect it differs entirely from the love scenes in
Romeo and Juliet. For on the island there is no priest, no
magistrate to marry them. There is not a line that suggests
union in the full marital sense. Perhaps this is what gives it
a sweetness that is unusual in other love scenes to be found
in our poet's plays.

The courtship of Ferdinand and Miranda matures without
caress or even a touch of the hand. When he tells her that
he is a king, she shows no surprise, and she does not interrupt
his speech to question him about his royal birth. He says:

> The very instant that I saw you, did
> My heart fly to your service; there resides,
> To make me slave to it; and for your sake
> Am I this patient log-man.

At this declaration she asks, "Do you love me?" The
simplicity of the question coming after his statement that he
is of royal birth reveals the nature of her spirit. Confessing
her own unworthiness, she tells him:

> I am your wife, if you will marry me;
> If not, I'll die your maid: to be your fellow
> You may deny me; but I'll be your servant,
> Whether you will or no.

Then their troth is plighted, and they pass from the scene.
This beautiful mating of two fine natures has been brought
about without spell cast by the magician and without the
agency of Ariel. It moves entirely upon the attraction gen-
erated by the natural impulse of each to adore the other.
This is just what lifts it up to a high plane of poetic fancy
and draws from us a pleasant feeling that love is something

more than what is implied in marriage and that the response
of two young hearts may be innocent of the joys and sorrows
of wedded life.

During this scene we are conscious that Prospero has
witnessed it all. Although we do not see him, we know he is
present. And now we are to learn what he thinks of it:

> So glad of this as they I cannot be,
> Who are surpris'd with all; but my rejoicing
> At nothing can be more. I'll to my book;
> For yet, ere supper-time, must I perform
> Much business appertaining.

The question that has always bothered the actor about
this speech is whether it should be given while he is unseen.
There is no necessity, after Miranda and Ferdinand leave the
scene, for Prospero to be in hiding. He might just as well
appear to speak the lines.

The one thing that interests me in this last short soliloquy
is the reference to work that must be undertaken before
supper-time. Prospero says, "I'll to my book," for there is
much business to perform.

We know that he had been engaged in secret studies before he left Milan and that the library Gonzalo put upon the
bark contained works that he valued higher than his dukedom. What were these books? Shakespeare must have had
in mind some of the tomes we discussed above.[2]

Our poet lived in the period when witchcraft was a burning topic, and raged fiercely in all parts of western Europe.
It is clear, however, that the art exercised by Prospero is not
to be confounded with that of the witches or any of their
kidney. He is a wizard who practices white magic for *good*
purposes.

Frank Kermode, in his introduction to the Arden edition
of *The Tempest*, deals with this matter in an exceedingly

[2] See chap. XII *supra*.

interesting manner, but he does not explain why it is necessary for Prospero to resort to his books, nor does he refer to
the titles of them. In a footnote he says:

> The book, so highly valued by Prospero and Cali-
> ban, as well as the rod, occur in all demonology, pop-
> ular and learned; they were required to be of virginal
> purity.[3]

This is strange, for I find nothing of demonology in Prospero's art. So far, no one has been injured through the exercise of his magical powers, although he has driven the ship
ashore in a gale that he has wrought up. The passengers and
the crew have been saved. As for Caliban, it would require
no magician's art to tame him or to make him do the necessary chores in supplying his master with wood and other
things. And the drunken bout of Stephano and the wine he
gives to Caliban need no aid from a magician.

The idea of a magician's art is no new expression in the
plays. The true magician is the poet, and in this respect the
author of *The Tempest* is perhaps personified in Prospero.

In the second scene of Act Three, we have an exhibition
of what civilized persons can do to deprave the savage. We
have already seen what was done by Prospero and Miranda,
during twelve years, to raise him from his state of nature to
that of a social being. Caliban's comment upon it indicates no
gratitude for his schooling. He says, "I know how to curse."

However, we should temper this confession by remember-
ing that Caliban has been dispossessed. Not only has Prospero
usurped his position as sole proprietor of the island, but he
has also cast the former ruler in the role of a common
drudge. Historically, such has been the fate of all native folk
whose lands have been visited by the educated adventurers
in search of treasure.

This may seem to the student a modern notion of the affair,

[3] P. xlix.

smacking of the imperialism of the seventeenth and eight-eenth centuries. Whatever difference there might be be-tween the work of Clive and Rhodes and that of Pizarro and Cortez may be argued to no advantage by the thin-skinned nationalists. Whether or not Shakespeare knew what had been done by the Spaniards in South America, he must have read the literature published in his day about the voyages and discoveries of the sea rovers. The experts make much of this point, and Frank Kermode deals with it at some length.

But apart from the knowledge he gained in that way, Shakespeare would have wit enough to compare Elizabethan methods with those recorded in pagan literature. He would have no qualms, such as our modern historians feel, about upsetting polite, conservative ideas behind the real missions of those who, in the name of civilization, desire to lift the native soul out of its darkness and flood it with Christian light.

Caliban, Stephano and Trinculo, in their drunken ramble, had wandered to another part of the island. Caliban has now been dubbed "Monsieur Monster" by Stephano. When the former ruler is called Moon-calf, he is ready to lick the shoe of his new master. Trinculo calls him "half a fish and half a monster."

But Caliban is not so drunk as to forget that a sorcerer "by his cunning hath cheated me of the island." And forth-with he puts before Stephano a plan to avenge the theft. He believes that Stephano will carry it out, and Caliban tells him: "Thou shalt be lord of it, and I'll serve thee."

The plot is to attack Prospero when he is asleep. Ariel, unseen, interrupts the conversation by interjecting that Cali-ban lies. Stephano and "Monsieur Monster" think the voice is that of Trinculo. There is no evidence in this scene that Ariel is carrying out the commands of Prospero. Yet Ariel might have wider functions than we imagined at first. The reason his voice is heard in this scene will appear later. The plan of revenge is laid before Stephano:

Why, as I told thee, 'tis a custom with him
I' th' afternoon to sleep: there thou mayst brain him,
Having first seiz'd his books; or with a log
Batter his skull, or paunch him with a stake,
Or cut his wezand with thy knife. Remember
First to possess his books; for without them
He's but a sot, as I am, nor hath not
One spirit to command: they all do hate him
As rootedly as I. Burn but his books.
He has brave utensils,—for so he calls them,—
Which, when he has a house, he'll deck withal.
And that most deeply to consider is
The beauty of his daughter; he himself
Calls her a nonpareil: I never saw a woman,
But only Sycorax my dam and she;
But she as far surpasseth Sycorax
As great'st does least.

Caliban tells Stephano that Miranda "will become thy bed, I warrant, and bring thee forth brave brood." The plot is to the liking of Stephano, who says, "I will kill this man: his daughter and I will be King and Queen." Such is the ambition of a drunken butler, and Trinculo, a very different jester from any other presented by Shakespeare, thinks the scheme "Excellent!"

They are so delighted that they sing the catch:

Flout 'em and scout 'em,
And scout 'em and flout 'em;
Thought is free.

Ariel then plays a tune on a tabor and pipe, and the music, coming from an unseen player, so frightens Stephano and Trinculo that they ask for mercy and forgiveness of sins. Caliban tells them not to be afraid, that the island is full of "sounds and sweet airs, that give delight, and hurt not." Stephano is soothed, and decides that it would be a brave kingdom for him and that he should have his music for nothing. But Caliban reminds him that that will not happen until Prospero is destroyed. They then decide to follow the music played by Ariel.

The use that Shakespeare makes of music in this play is deserving of our consideration. *The Tempest* gives us a lesson in the power of music as an anesthetic, as well as a means of raising souls from the sloughs of depression. Plato, in some of the finest passages of the *Republic*, deals with the efficacy of music as a refining medium for man. John Burnet, in *Early Greek Philosophy*, tells us: "Aristoxenos said that the Pythagoreans employed music to purge the soul as they used medicine to purge the body." [4]

How often in Shakespeare's plays is music called for for this purpose. He must have realized that music is the highest form of the refining arts. It is the spiritual means of ennobling the creature. Whether by the voice of the singer or the string of the lyre, by Pan's pipe or Triton's horn, it is universal in its effect on human creatures; and the marvel of it is, it can be gay or sad, a wedding march or a funeral dirge; it can set the feet of a maiden dancing a jig; it can provoke laughter or flood the eyes with tears. What can it not do to disperse the shadows that fall into every life? Bach's idea was: "The aim and final reason of all music should be nothing else but the glory of God and the refreshment of the spirit." One of its miracles is noted in *The Tempest*, for it reached the soul of Caliban.

Few of the critics have attempted to explain Caliban's desire that Stephano should take Prospero's books before they kill him. It is a most startling idea, for Caliban tells his newly found friends that Prospero is but a sot without them. He insists: "Burn but his books."

Has the education of Caliban been of such an order that he believes it is from books that Prospero has learned to

[4] Fourth ed.; London: A. & C. Black, 1930, p. 97.

exercise magical powers? We can imagine that the former proprietor of the island, during the twelve years of his education and serfdom, has often seen Prospero at his secret studies. We may take it that in Prospero's library there were no books for schoolboys, no primers, no first steps to learning. Therefore, Caliban must have received an oral schooling. To such a creature, books would have a somewhat mysterious value, and the script would seem to have an indefinable power that would give the scholar a mystical influence.

This is not so strange as it might seem. I can well imagine that people in England in Shakespeare's day who had never gone to school would regard the books of the time as strange talismans, containing perhaps the secrets of demonology and witchcraft. When I was a boy, an old Sanskrit scholar—an aged bundle of love and kindness to all about him—was feared because no one who saw his books could read the script. Yes, even before the turn of the twentieth century, there were people in England who imagined there was something "not quite regular" (to use their expression) about books written in an alien script.

So, for Caliban to say that Prospero, without his books, is but a sot indicates that he attributes his magical powers to the information he gathers from them. Caliban knows nothing of Ariel. Although the latter had been confined in the split pine by his mother, he does not know of his existence, and it is not difficult for us to understand why all the offices performed by the creative imagination in action seem to Caliban to derive from information gathered from the books.

Alonso, Gonzalo and others of the King's company have wandered far into another part of the island. They have been in quest of Ferdinand, fearful that the terrible bulls and lions, whose roaring woke Sebastian and Antonio, might

devour the heir to the throne of Naples. Gonzalo is footsore
and weary and asks for time to rest. Alonso, too, is tired of
the search. He gives up hope of finding Ferdinand.

> . . . . He is drown'd
> Whom thus we stray to find; and the sea mocks
> Our frustrate search on land. Well, let him go.

The plan to kill the King and his councellor was frustrated
when Ariel sang in Gonzalo's ear and woke him to find
Antonio and Sebastian with their swords drawn. Now while
Alonso and Gonzalo rest their wearied bodies, the conspirators determine to carry out their plan when the next opportunity comes:

> Ant. [Aside to Seb.] Let it be to-night;
> For, now they are oppress'd with travel, they
> Will not, nor cannot, use such vigilance
> As when they are fresh.
> Seb. [Aside to Ant.] I say, to-night: no more.

The reader should bear in mind, in this scene, that Sebastian is the brother of Alonso, whom he intends Antonio to
slay. And Antonio is the brother of Prospero, and had cast
him and his child adrift. There is no such association among
the other conspirators. Neither Caliban nor Stephano is re-
lated to other characters in the play.

Then comes an exhibition of magic, which reminds us of
the conjuring acts performed by Maskelyne and Houdini.
There is solemn and haunting music. Prospero is present but
invisible. Strange creatures appear, bringing in a banquet
set upon a table. They act the part of waiters, bowing and
scraping, and with gestures inviting the King and the others
to eat. Then they depart.

Alonso is so startled he calls on the heavens to give them
kind keepers, and Sebastian calls it a living drollery and says
he can believe there are unicorns. Gonzalo is sure that, if he
reported such a thing in Naples, people would doubt him.

Still, in his comment about it, there is a satirical reference to the story of islanders brought home by the sea rovers.

If I should say, I saw such islanders,—
For, certes, these are people of the island,—
Who, though they are of monstrous shape, yet, note,
Their manners are more gentle, kind, than of
Our human generation you shall find
Many, nay, almost any.

Upon this we hear Prospero say, "Honest lord, thou hast said well; for some of you there present are worse than devils." After they have discussed the wonder of this phenomenon, thunder and lightning burst forth, and Ariel, like a harpy, claps his wings upon the table and the banquet vanishes.

Then in denouncing them, Ariel tells them, "You are three men of sin." And when they draw their swords, he says, "You fools! I and my fellows are ministers of Fate."

Ariel reminds them of their deeds, saying:

. . . . You three
From Milan did supplant good Prospero:
Expos'd unto the sea, which hath requit it,
Him and his innocent child: for which foul deed
The powers, delaying, not forgetting, have
Incens'd the seas and shores, yea, all the creatures,
Against your peace. . . . .

The imps of the banquet enter again and dance; and then with mocks and bows carry out the table. Prospero leaves the scene, with his enemies now in his power. They are bewildered, stricken with fear and in a nervous condition. Alonso thinks "the thunder, that deep and dreadful organ-pipe, pronounc'd the name of Prosper." After Alonso, Sebastian and Antonio have left the scene, Gonzalo brings it to an end:

All three of them are desperate: their great guilt,
Like poison given to work a great time after,
Now 'gins to bite the spirits. . . . .

Sixteen

ACT FOUR—THE MASQUE

We find Prospero, Ferdinand, and Miranda before the cell. It is the same setting as the second scene in the first act. The stage has now been reached in the courtship of the two lovers when Prospero is ready to decide their future. He says to Ferdinand:

> Then, as my gift, and thine own acquisition
> Worthily purchas'd, take my daughter: but
> If thou dost break her virgin-knot before
> All sanctimonious ceremonies may
> With full and holy rite be minister'd,
> No sweet aspersion shall the heavens let fall
> To make this contract grow; but barren hate,
> Sour-ey'd disdain and discord shall bestrew
> The union of your bed with weeds so loathly
> That you shall hate it both: therefore take heed,
> As Hymen's lamps shall light you.[1]

This means that Prospero has no power to unite them. They shall have to wait until there is a priest to perform the ceremony. The magician may have power over the elements, matter and secular things, but the religious realm is barred to him. I consider this one of the most revealing comments on Shakespeare's mature thoughts about the sanctity of wedded life. It is his conviction that order must be preserved in all things that are to endure. Happiness depends upon a right beginning.

[1] The quotations in this chapter are from Act IV.

Exacting the promise from Ferdinand that he will keep Miranda chaste until a religious ceremony can be performed surely means that Prospero is confident he will return to Italy. Ariel enters, and Prospero orders him to be of use in another trick, saying:

> . . . . Go bring the rabble,
> O'er whom I give thee power, here to this place:
> Incite them to quick motion; for I must
> Bestow upon the eyes of this young couple
> Some vanity of mine Art; it is my promise,
> And they expect it from me.

There is then presented a scene so beautiful in its sentiment, color, and purpose that many readers may wonder why it finds a place in *The Tempest*. Several of the Shakespearian scholars believe it was especially written for the performance that was given at the time of the marriage of King James' daughter, Elizabeth, to Prince Palatine. Some think it was introduced after the play had been written. To my mind, this piece is foreshadowed in the speech of Gonzalo, already referred to.[2] It is undoubtedly rich in ideas of the Golden Age. It harks back to Hesiod and Pindar and the Isles of the Blest, as well as to the *Critias* of Plato.

Such thoughts of economic paradise have haunted the minds of men ever since *Works and Days* was written. And Shakespeare's memory was still fresh about the things he had heard as a boy from his father and the tales his grandfather told. How many passages are there in the plays that remind us of this, not only in the histories but in the comedies? And who had greater reason to wish for a return of the days when barns were full, and people happy, than those who lived during the reigns of the Tudors?

Ceres puts the seal on this memory:

> Earth's increase, foison plenty,
> Barns and garners never empty;

[2] *Supra*, chap XIV.

Vines with clust'ring bunches growing;
Plants with goodly burthen bowing;
Spring come to you at the farthest
In the very end of harvest!
Scarcity and want shall shun you;
Ceres' blessing so is on you.

This symbolic picture of the desires of the folk could only have been written by a poet who knew the country and had the smell of the soil in his nostrils. Then, when the reapers and nymphs have danced, Prospero suddenly becomes aware, by some magical means, of the plot of Caliban against his life, and everything disappears. He is wrought into a great passion, which amazes Ferdinand and Miranda. He tells them not to be dismayed, but that the revels are now ended. And with the passing of the goddesses, fairies and reapers, Prospero is left with the realities of existence. Actuality pierces keenly the intuitions and imaginations of the poet, which give to "airy nothing a local habitation and a name." Yes, such tricks have strong imagination, and they undoubtedly do conjure up some joy, if only for the moment they are visualized by the poet.

Shakespeare knew that actuality could not be narrowed to fit into a one-way groove. Life is a thronged thoroughfare, and up and down it pass beauty and ugliness, virtue and vice. From Ceres to Caliban is a startling change of theme.

The gathering of the goddesses on the "short-grass'd green" before the cell of Prospero is not only a graceful interlude; it is, besides, a blessing of hope that both the lovers of the play and of the court shall enjoy the riches of earth. It is a vision of the ideal island Gonzalo pictured earlier in the play. Where our poet found the idea he has enhanced I do not know, but it seems to me that it might have been inspired by Hesiod.

Here are some of the lines from *Works and Days:*

. . . . [There was once] a golden race of mortal men.
. . . . They lived like gods without sorrow of heart,
remote and free from toil and grief. . . . . They had
all good things; for the fruitful earth unforced bare
them fruit abundantly and without stint. They dwelt
in ease and peace upon their lands with many good
things, rich in flocks and loved by the blessed gods.[3]

There is also a reference to the Islands of the Blest, where
"they live untouched by sorrow," and "the grain-giving
earth bears honey-sweet fruit flourishing thrice a year." [4]

It is a story of the bounteous earth yielding abundance
for her creatures. Hesiod tells us, "Neither famine nor disaster ever haunt men who do true justice," [5] and that "he
does mischief to himself who does mischief to another, and
evil planned harms the plotter most." [6]

These people of the Fortunate Isles never knew empty
barns, and Ceres wished for the lovers "barns and garners
never empty." It really does seem as if Shakespeare might
have dramatized a page from Hesiod.

In some of the *Odes*, Pindar also speaks of this happy race,
who were exempt from disease or old age, from toils and
warfare:

> They need not the moon in that land of delight,
>   They need not the pale, pale star;
> The sun is bright, by day and night,
> Where the souls of the blessed are.
>
> They till not the ground, they plow not the wave,
>   They labor not, never! oh, never!
> Not a tear do they shed, not a sigh do they heave;
> They are happy for ever and ever! [7]

[3] Trans. by Hugh G. Evelyn-White, Loeb Classical Library (London: Wm. Heinemann; N.Y.: Macmillan, 1914), p. 11.
[4] *Ibid.*, p. 15.
[5] *Ibid.*, p. 21.
[6] *Ibid.*, p. 23.
[7] As quoted in Bulfinch's *Age of Fable* (Philadelphia: David McKay,
1898), p. 3.

The island described in the *Timaeus* was surely not one of the Islands of the Blest. It was Atlantis, a great military power that "endeavored to subdue at one blow our country and yours and the whole of the land which was within the straits." [8]

In the *Critias* we have the description of a different people, but they are quite unlike those described by Hesiod. Still, the fertility of the land and its beauty give it an attraction for those who wish to live under ideal circumstances. There are many references to conditions similar to those alluded to by Juno and Ceres.

Herodotus, in Chapter IV of his *History*—"Melpomene" —describes the life of the Hyperboreans. These were the people who lived in a land of perpetual sunshine and great fertility. They knew not disease nor war, and they lived a thousand years.

This visit of Iris, Juno and Ceres enchants Ferdinand, and he says to Prospero:

> Let me live here ever;
> So rare a wonder'd father and a wise
> Makes this place Paradise.

The wish for an economic paradise inspired Prospero to extend his art beyond shipwreck, taming Caliban, bringing his enemies to his feet, and even conjuring a banquet table attended by impish waiters. In this, he projected his powers as far as high Olympus and brought the rainbow from the sky to assist Ceres in rejoicing the hearts of the lovers. It is not out of place, and it would be a fitting interlude in the play, whether a royal marriage was about to be celebrated or not.

What interests me in considering the works Shakespeare must have been familiar with is the wide scope we find not only in *The Tempest* but in several of the other works. I

[8] *The Works of Plato*, trans. by Jowett, IV, 370.

have already spoken of an edition of *Works and Days* published in 1493, and the complete works were brought out in Venice two years later. That he browsed in many classical fields of knowledge no one can deny. In *Hamlet* he names many of the pagan gods, men and women.

Whether he knew Greek or not, he must have been in close association with someone who was a scholar. The language question so often raised by the experts presents no difficulty for me, for we have so many instances of the rapidity with which well-known people have mastered foreign tongues. Henry Schliemann was one who mastered modern Greek in six weeks, and in the next six months, enough ancient Greek to read the *Iliad* and *Odyssey* with the most lively enthusiasm. We also have the testimony of the great Rudolph Virchow concerning this fact. He wrote to Schliemann saying he had learned the classical languages in the same way.[9]

Another instance of mastering Greek in a short time is that of a German professor at one of our chief universities. He told me that, by a special method used after World War I, he became proficient enough after eight months of intensive work to receive his degree.

We have been in the clouds, drifting pleasantly over high Olympus. But no poet or anyone he charms can stay there for long. The descent to earth, even for the Prosperos, unfortunately, does not always set one down on the Islands of the Blest. Earth is no myth. Ceres and Juno may indulge in transports of promise upon the patch in front of Prospero's cell, but when they depart, we find that life is not only real but sinister, in many of its aspects. We are brought up harshly against reality, and the task it presents to us must be undertaken, or we surrender the modicum of freedom that we cherish.

[9] See Virchow's letter in *Ilios*, by Henry Schliemann (N.Y.: Harper, 1881), p. 15.

Life in its constant round of small hopes and great afflictions is nothing but a humiliating compromise with opposites. Evil is no lone traveler. It is never far from the elbow of good. No one revealed a deeper knowledge of this distressing fact than Shakespeare. The illustrations of it in *The Tempest* are startling when we recognize the close association of exalted virtue and sheer depravity. Miranda and Caliban, Prospero and Antonio, Ferdinand and Stephano, Gonzalo and Sebastian are contrasts that remind us of many Old Testament texts: "It is better to hear the rebuke of the wise, than for a man to hear the song of fools." [10]

Natural goodness shines in the character of Miranda. The world has not touched her. But Nature in the raw, as shown in Caliban, cannot be tamed and trained by the intellect, even that of Prospero. This sad reflection upon the futility of trying to inculcate goodness in creatures not ready to take it is more poignant when we realize how often educated people have succumbed to the urge of gaining power, wealth, or even fame, by devious acts.

From dreams of an earthly paradise we awaken to find ourselves confronted with the ugly facts of existence. Ariel has forgotten to report to Prospero the plan of Caliban and Stephano to murder him in his sleep, but we may assume the magician has learned of it by telepathy.

This new manifestation of depravity makes him realize the perversity and disorder of the mind of man. The dreams of a better state of affairs are worthless, and he says to Ferdinand:

> These our actors,
> As I foretold you, were all spirits, and
> Are melted into air, into thin air:
> And, like the baseless fabric of this vision,
> The cloud-capp'd towers, the gorgeous palaces,
> The solemn temples, the great globe itself,

[10] Eccles. 7:5.

> Yea, all which it inherit, shall dissolve,
> And, like this insubstantial pageant faded,
> Leave not a rack behind. . . . .

A discouraging picture of the future for a young lover, who, no doubt, is already building his castles in the air, in which he will live in peace and happiness with his bride. But he is reminded by Prospero that:

> . . . . We are such stuff
> As dreams are made on; and our little life
> Is rounded with a sleep. . . . .

Yet, youth without hope would mean a barren life. And there hope resides, as though it were under the rim of Pandora's box. Still, the miseries that escaped on earth are abroad day and night, and now Prospero knows it keenly. He is vexed and asks Ferdinand to bear with his weakness. His old brain is troubled, and he seeks exercise and air to still his throbbing mind. What a scene is this! Coming after the fantasy of the goddesses, it is a disheartening event, for it really means that the work of twelve years, in trying to civilize Caliban, has been thrown away.

Shakespeare was a mentor who never let us indulge in baseless fantasies. Even in the comedies of happy ending, we are left with the thought that all is well for the time being. That it ends well is sufficient for the denouement of a comedy, but we are not deceived, though we have been pleasantly entertained.

The desire of a Henry VI to change places with the shepherd who watches his silly sheep is a thought that lies at the core of Shakespeare's reasoning upon the strange contrariness that afflicts all but those who are bound to the soil. The Golden Age, the Isles of the Blest, the Hyperboreans are stories of ideals of existence that have sunk deeply into the memories of man. Better little and no cares than power and wealth.

> . . . . Who would fardels bear,
> To grunt and sweat under a weary life,
> But that the dread of something after death,
> The undiscover'd country from whose bourn
> No traveller returns, puzzles the will,
> And makes us rather bear those ills we have
> Than fly to others we know not of?[11]

Prospero, left alone, calls for Ariel and tells him they must prepare to meet Caliban. His spirit has taken the drunken conspirators far afield "through tooth'd briers, sharp furzes, pricking goss, and thorns" and then led them into a filthy-mantled pool. Prospero orders Ariel to bring the rich garments from the cell for the purpose of tempting the drunken thieves. Ariel leaves to fulfill the errand. Alone again, Prospero reflects upon the work of twelve years devoted to civilizing Caliban.

The magician has to admit defeat, and does so in words that other reformers have used:

> A devil, a born devil, on whose nature
> Nurture can never stick; on whom my pains,
> Humanely taken, all, all lost, quite lost;
> And as with age his body uglier grows,
> So his mind cankers. I will plague them all,
> Even to roaring.

Ariel enters with the glistering garments, and Prospero bids him hang them on the line. Then, hearing the approach of the drunken trio, the magician and his spirit become invisible. Stephano and Trinculo blame Caliban for playing jack-o'-lantern with them. They have lost their bottles. They are still under the influence of the liquor, and Caliban is in disgrace. All he can do is remind them of their plan:

> *Cal.* Prithee, my King, be quiet. Sees' thou here,
> This is the mouth o' th' cell: no noise, and enter.
> Do that good mischief which may make this island

[11] *Hamlet*, Act III, scene 1.

> Thine own for ever, and I, thy Caliban,
> For aye thy foot-licker.
>   *Ste.* Give me thy hand. I do begin to have bloody
> thoughts.
>   *Trin.* O King Stephano! O peer! O worthy Ste-
> phano! look what a wardrobe here is for thee!
>   *Cal.* Let it alone, thou fool; it is but trash.
>   *Trin.* O, ho, monster! we know what belongs to a
> frippery. O King Stephano!

Trinculo takes a gown from the line and puts it on, and
he and Stephano quarrel about who shall have it. They fight
over the gaudy clothes and beat Caliban. Suddenly there is
a noise of hunters calling upon dogs, and spirits in the shape
of hounds come hunting about the scuffling conspirators.
Prospero and Ariel, unseen, set the dogs onto them, and
they are driven out. They are heard roaring in panic as they
fly away. As the sound dies, Prospero realizes

> . . . . At this hour
> Lies at my mercy all mine enemies:
> Shortly shall all my labours end, and thou
> Shalt have the air at freedom: for a little
> Follow, and do me service.

There is something in this scene that reminds me of the
Twenty-second Psalm:

> For dogs have compassed me: the assembly of the
> wicked have inclosed me. . . . .
> They part my garments among them. . . . .
> Deliver my soul from the sword; my darling from
> the power of the dog.[12]

The punishment meted out to the conspirators seems to
be no more severe than if a gamekeeper set his dogs upon
some poachers. And it is also strange that they should be
used for the purpose. In the Old and New Testaments, this

---

[12] Vss. 16, 18, 20.

animal was placed among the unclean beasts, and traffic in it was regarded as an abomination.

Perhaps the reader of the play is not aware of the problem of punishment presented in it. But on the stage, when the curtain falls on the fourth act, the audience cannot fail to wonder what Prospero will do with his enemies, now that he has them in his power. How will they be punished for their misdeeds? That is the question that will arise in every mind, and it will seem that Prospero has let off lightly Caliban and his two friends. Hence, the fifth act is one in which the audience expects Prospero to avenge himself upon his brother and the Duke of Milan.

Seventeen

ACT FIVE—RECONCILIATION

Prospero comes from his cell dressed in his magic robes, and Ariel follows him. He asks the spirit, "How fares the King and 's followers?" The reply is that they are in such sorrow and dismay that, if Prospero could see them, his affections would become tender. This is a revelation; indeed, it is a most unexpected turn in the drama that Ariel should be the one to remind the magician that the suffering of his enemies, under his charm, afflicts them so strongly that he would become tender if he saw them.

> *Pros.* Dost thou think so, spirit?
> *Ari.* Mine would, sir, were I human.
> *Pros.* And mine shall.
> Hast thou, which art but air, a touch, a feeling
> Of their afflictions, and shall not myself,
> One of their kind, that relish all as sharply
> Passion as they, be kindlier mov'd than thou art?
> Though with their high wrongs I am struck to th' quick,
> Yet with my nobler reason 'gainst my fury
> Do I take part: the rarer action is
> In virtue than in vengeance: they being penitent,
> The sole drift of my purpose doth extend
> Not a frown further. Go release them, Ariel:
> My charms I'll break, their senses I'll restore,
> And they shall be themselves.[1]

"The rarer action is in virtue than in vengeance." This change of intention startles us. The idea suggested by Ariel

[1] All quotations in this chapter are from Act V, unless otherwise noted.

has taken root, and the magician realizes the impotence of earthly punishment.

Shakespeare had given to us the record of crimes committed by Angevins, Plantagenets, Tudors and the rabble throngs of their reigns. He knew the history of all the punishment that man can invent. The record covered royal vengeance, judgments of the Star Chamber, the decrees of Parliament, the rack, the stake, the gallows and the gibbets of Catholic and Protestant displeasure. And what did it all avail? Was anyone the better for it, anyone blessed? It seemed as if the more punishment, the more crime was bred. Why, therefore, persist in a system of murder for murder, when there seemed to be no end to it—no happier day?

He sends Ariel to fetch Alonso, Antonio and the others to him. The spirit leaves him alone, and in a soliloquy of superlative grandeur, he distills the philosophy of his art:

> Ye elves of hills, brooks, standing lakes, and groves;
> And ye that on the sands with printless foot
> Do chase the ebbing Neptune, and do fly him
> When he comes back; you demi-puppets that
> By moonshine do the green sour ringlets make,
> Whereof the ewe not bites; and you whose pastime
> Is to make midnight mushrooms, that rejoice
> To hear the solemn curfew; by whose aid—
> Weak masters though ye be—I have bedimm'd
> The noontide sun, call'd forth the mutinous winds,
> And 'twixt the green sea and the azur'd vault
> Set roaring war: to the dread rattling thunder
> Have I given fire, and rifted Jove's stout oak
> With his own bolt; the strong-bas'd promontory
> Have I made shake, and by the spurs pluck'd up
> The pine and cedar: graves at my command
> Have wak'd their sleepers, op'd, and let 'em forth
> By my so potent Art. But this rough magic
> I here abjure; and, when I have requir'd
> Some heavenly music,—which even now I do,—
> To work mine end upon their senses, that

This airy charm is for, I'll break my staff,
Bury it certain fadoms in the earth,
And deeper than did ever plummet sound
I'll drown my book.

In bidding farewell to his art, he asks for "some heavenly music." We know the part that music has already played in this drama. It has bewitched the most degraded specimens the poet has put in his plays. Even Stephano has been affected by it, and Caliban has good words for it.

I often wonder what the cults would have done without music. The power of the instrument, whether it be the harp, lute or organ, is soul-cleansing. And in many of the plays, Shakespeare uses it as an anodyne in several scenes.

There are passages in the speeches of Prospero and Ariel that seem to be somewhat alien to their characters. And in the speech quoted above, I find references to ideas and fancies that are peculiarly English. Take, for example, the one about "demi-puppets that by moonshine do the green sour ringlets make, whereof the ewe not bites; and you whose pastime is to make midnight mushrooms." In the heart of Shropshire, boys pointed out these ringlets to me in pastures when I was not more than seven years old. And I have known my grandmother to go out and pick midnight mushrooms when the dew would be so heavy that she would wear pattens to keep her feet dry.

I cannot imagine Prospero as the Duke of Milan or the magician of the isle noting these evidences of the work of the elves. These are fancies of people of the soil, and many a beautiful myth has been woven about the elves sheltering themselves under a field mushroom, whose spread is flat, sheltering there when the dew was falling heavily. These were the elves that made the rings and soured the grass that the sheep would not nibble. There is so much in *The Tempest* of Shakespeare himself, who knew the meads, the ditches, the wild flowers, the birds, and the kine, and which reveals a direct and intimate knowledge of the countryside.

The scene that follows is in the nature of a confession of the impotence of condign punishment. Ariel has entered, bringing Prospero's enemies before him. They stand in a charmed circle, spell-stopp'd. After giving thanks to Gonzalo, "my true preserver," he reminds the others of their offenses. He says, "Unnatural though thou art, I do forgive thee." Then, so that they may know in whose power they stand, Prospero tells Ariel:

> Fetch me the hat and rapier in my cell:
> I will discase me, and myself present
> As I was sometime Milan: quickly, spirit;
> Thou shalt ere long be free.

As he helps him to dress in the clothing of Milan, Ariel sings:

> Where the bee sucks, there suck I:
> In a cowslip's bell I lie;
> There I couch when owls do cry.
> On the bat's back I do fly
> After summer merrily.
> Merrily, merrily shall I live now
> Under the blossom that hangs on the bough.

This smacks more of Snitterfield than it does of Caliban's island. Is it so strange that nostalgic thoughts should come flooding into the poet's mind at this period of his career?

After the song, Ariel is dispatched to make the ship and the crew ready for the passage. Then Prospero reveals himself. He embraces Gonzalo and gives his company a hearty welcome. They are not convinced, and Alonso asks for particulars of his preservation. After establishing his identity to the satisfaction of his former enemies, he welcomes them, saying, "This cell's my court."

Prospero discovers Ferdinand and Miranda playing chess, and Alonso finds Ferdinand. The climacteric is reached, when enemies and friends are harmoniously united in the love of the young couple:

Alon. Now all the blessings
Of a glad father compass thee about!
Arise, and say how thou cam'st here.
   Mir. O, wonder!
How many goodly creatures are there here!
How beauteous mankind is! O brave new world,
That has such people in 't!
   Pros. 'Tis new to thee.
   Alon. What is this maid with whom thou wast at play?
Your eld'st acquaintance cannot be three hours:
Is she the goddess that hath sever'd us,
And brought us thus together?
   Fer. Sir, she is mortal;
But by immortal Providence she's mine:
I chose her when I could not ask my father
For his advice, nor thought I had one. She
Is daughter to this famous Duke of Milan,
Of whom so often I have heard renown,
But never saw before; of whom I have
Receiv'd a second life; and second father
This lady makes him to me.

Here another magician has been at work: the human heart
beating in harmony with the spheres; the throbs of joy, like
the rays of the risen sun, piercing the chilly dews of night.
Perhaps in this we may find that there is a punishment, even
in forgiveness. We say, as they said then, "Forgive us our
trespasses as we forgive those who trespass against us," but
so far as we know, Prospero had no sins to be forgiven. His
position is unique. It may be in the inscrutable workings of
the laws of the universe that there is a punishment of the
soul, which is far more effective than that of man-made laws.
For, to forgive one's enemies may be an act that recoils on
them in a purely spiritual way. It may lead to contrition, and
abject atonement may be the means to redemption.

But that is no more than a medieval idea. Yet, the old records tell us many a story of what spiritual penance has done
to reclaim a soul that might have been lost. Again, I must

remark that this is a play concerning the impotence of the laws made by man for punishing crime. There is no sanctuary now.

Ariel comes with the master of the ship and all is arranged for a return to Milan and Naples. But Caliban and his drunken companions remain to be dealt with, and Ariel brings them before Prospero and the others. They are still under the influence of liquor, but not so drunk that they do not realize they are in the presence of their master. They sober up when they learn that their conspiracy is known to Prospero. He then turns to Caliban:

> . . . . Go, sirrah, to my cell;
> Take with you your companions; as you look
> To have my pardon, trim it handsomely.
>   *Cal.* Ay, that I will; and I'll be wise hereafter,
> And seek for grace. What a thrice-double ass
> Was I, to take this drunkard for a god,
> And worship this dull fool!

The conversion of the son of Sycorax is a speedy one, and that exceptionally searching critic, Ernest Renan, in his *Caliban et l'Eau de Jouvence*,[2] gives us a most amusing sequel to the return of Prospero and Caliban to Milan.

The end draws near, and Prospero invites the redeemed ones to his cell, where he will tell them the story of how he came to the isle. Next morning they will embark for Naples,

> Where I have hope to see the nuptial
> Of these our dear-belov'd solemnized;
> And thence retire me to my Milan, where
> Every third thought shall be my grave.

For Ariel the moment of his freedom is at hand. Prospero charges him to arrange for calm seas, and then "to the elements be free, and fare you well."

The epilogue spoken by Prospero is a renunciation of the

[2] Paris: Calmann-Levy, 1925.

art of the magician. His charms are all overthrown, and now he can rely only upon his own native strength. However, for the future he has a wish of an ideal condition for men, which resides in the heart of the true philosopher:

> Now I want
> Spirits to enforce, Art to enchant;
> And my ending is despair,
> Unless I be reliev'd by prayer,
> Which pierces so, that it assaults
> Mercy itself, and frees all faults.
>> As you from crimes would pardon'd be,
>> Let your indulgence set me free.[3]

His realization of the efficacy of the prayer of a contrite heart is one of the finest tokens of his philosophy.

Whether or not this play is autobiographical, in some respects, we may take it that it is a summing up of all the distressing conflicts and turbulence that wracked Shakespeare's mind and spirit. The hope for a new age must have been dominant in his mind when he wrote *The Tempest*, but it was the tempest in his own soul that prompted him to create Prospero.

[3] Epilogue.

Eighteen

A MESSAGE OF THE PLAY

In SUMMARY, we might reconsider the somewhat cryptic matter of what was Shakespeare's intention in writing *The Tempest*. In the masque there is not a religious or political note sounded. Its ideas are celestial and economic—a lyric symphony of the seasons of growth, of fruit and of harvest. The joys of earth's blessings are to be showered upon the lovers. A Golden Age of riches will come to them, with children who will honor their parents. Ceres calls for "Earth's increase, foison plenty, barns and garners never empty."

The political state, as it was known to Prospero, is forgotten. The strivings for power, the quarrels of royal aspirants, the rise and fall of dynasties have no place in the future of Ferdinand and Miranda. There is not even a hint that the heir to Naples will take the throne. Royalty would die for want of pomp and tribute where "sunburn'd sicklemen, of August weary" dance in joyous mirth. "Let me live here ever," Ferdinand proclaims. "This short-grass'd green" has become a paradise. To him it has been a vision of the conditions prevailing in the Isles of the Blest, but to the intellectual, philosophical Prospero a mere dream broken by actuality.

> . . . . Let me not,
> Since I have my dukedom got,

> And pardon'd the deceiver, dwell
> In this bare island. . . . .

he prays in the epilogue. That is the saddest note of all, for forgiveness and redemption are brittle virtues and often have short life, and no one knows this fact as well as he does. For him, divested of his magical power, even though he should resume his "secret studies," life in Milan would be an uncertain business after the rule of Antonio.

Before Prospero was cast adrift by his brother, his "library was dukedom large enough." He is now twelve years older. His "old brain is troubled," and he asks Ferdinand to bear with his weakness. What lot has fortune marked out for him?

The future of Prospero in Milan will depend upon the political and social conditions he will find there on his return. His brother, Antonio, is silent. No word of contrition is spoken by him. And Sebastian reveals no sign of sorrow for his sin. Redemption, then, concerns only Alonso and Caliban. The King confesses his fault before he learns that Ferdinand is alive. He says to Prospero:

> Thy dukedom I resign, and do entreat
> Thou pardon me my wrongs. . . . .

Here remorse is shown and confession made prior to the grant of pardon. This is according to the way it is expressed in the Lord's Prayer. Contrition and forgiveness are inseparably bound. Redemption is then a fulfillment and the grant of pardon justified.

How strange that Caliban should be the other, of all the rest, to feel the pang of guilt and make a plea for grace. This is a most astonishing reformation. In Caliban, the son of Sycorax, the promptings of sorrow are felt; but no regrets, no words of shame come from Antonio and Sebastian. Still, we may be sure Prospero does not hoodwink himself about his future in Milan.

When his creator wrote the speech, which comes after the revels of the masque, he pointed directly to the pleasing fallacy which prompts us to indulge in fancies about a political state, in which rule will be just and order maintained by the good will of its citizens. For three or four thousand years our renowned philosophers have given deep thought to such a system. The reply is: "We are such stuff as dreams are made on." The reality is history. All such imaginings "shall dissolve, and, like the insubstantial pageant faded, leave not a rack behind."

> Gives not the hawthorn bush a sweeter shade
> To shepherds, looking on their silly sheep,
> Than doth a rich embroider'd canopy
> To kings, that fear their subjects' treachery?

In this we find the *leitmotif* which runs through most of the plays. It announces a return to primary affairs—call it the simple life, if you will; yet it cannot be ignored, and only one who wrote the verse for Ceres in the masque could use this theme repeatedly as a dominant in the scale of his artistry. Shakespeare is impregnated with the ideas of Utopia. In many respects he is Raphael Hythloday turned dramatist.

We may search here and there in play after play for a clue to his intention. Frank Kermode quotes D. G. James on this problem:

> Shakespeare, having failed to see human life as a neat, orderly, and satisfying unity, had resort to myth for conveyance of his new imaginative apprehension of life.[1]

Why new? Life was real to him when he wrote *Henry VI*. He had seen so much of it then that he gave one of the characters this line: "I would be well content to entertain the lag-end of my life with quiet hours." In what way do the

[1] *Loc. cit.*, p. lxxxv.

iniquities of the enemies of Prospero differ from the crimes of the Platagenets and Tudors?

Shakespeare's "apprehension of life" was not knowledge which came to him suddenly and prompted him to write *The Tempest*. What was new in idea and artistry was Prospero, the magician, who was vested with supernatural ideas and could command the service of an Ariel—a spirit—to carry out the schemes he was unable to execute.

If there be intention in the play, it must lie in a philosophic interpretation of the plot. Therein it is possible to glean a notion of the impotence of man, subject of a political state, to rule himself; and that a higher power is essential to set him free from "a foul and pestilential congregation of vapors."

Critics who have labored in vain to give to this play symbolic ideas of mercy, redemption, and, in some cases, Christian doctrine, overlook the text which is quite plain if read with sense and understanding, as Ezra remarked about the Law. Those who imagine the theme concerns "the recovery of lost royalty by a royal personage" wander far beyond the precise information found in the text.

Let us pause, for a moment or two, to trace the ideas relative to kingdoms and dukedoms. Prospero was a student and preferred his library to the council chamber. Ferdinand tells Miranda he is a prince; "I do think, a King; I would not so!" To be with her, he is content to be her "patient log-man." In Act V, Gonzalo, a royal councellor, the perfect courtier, says:

> Was Milan thrust from Milan, that his issue
> Should become Kings of Naples?

and he rejoices because Claribel found a husband in Tunis, Ferdinand found a wife on the isle, and Prospero regained his dukedom. There is no response to this from King or Duke. To them it is of so little importance that Alonso takes the hands of the lovers and wishes them joy. The attitude of

Prospero was expressed clearly in the same scene when he said:

> Let us not burthen our remembrance with
> A heaviness that's gone.

It is only Gonzalo who thinks of thrones and crowns.

The love match is so novel, so pure, that it soars in interest far above the trappings of a court. Miranda is as near Nature in spring garment as any heroine created by poet. She is an open-air maid, and has not known a lady-in-waiting for twelve years. She does not imagine there is such a place as a boudoir.

And how does Prospero regard the return to his dukedom? After the marriage in Naples, he will depart—

> . . . . Retire me to my Milan, where
> Every third thought shall be my grave.

No word of ducal rule, of political reform, of pomp and circumstance. Quite the reverse, indeed, is his last hope:

> . . . . Now I want
> Spirits to enforce, Art to enchant. . . . .

The mind that created Hamlet created Prospero. The indecision of the Prince of Denmark is the indecision of man, "sicklied o'er with the pale cast of thought." Hence, a play to give us hope, to turn our minds to higher values that the state knows not of, to forsake the beaten path of man's inhumanity to man, and to seek the essentials of life; as Timon puts it, "the bounteous housewife," the Nature-Mother of us all.